TALES OF BURMA

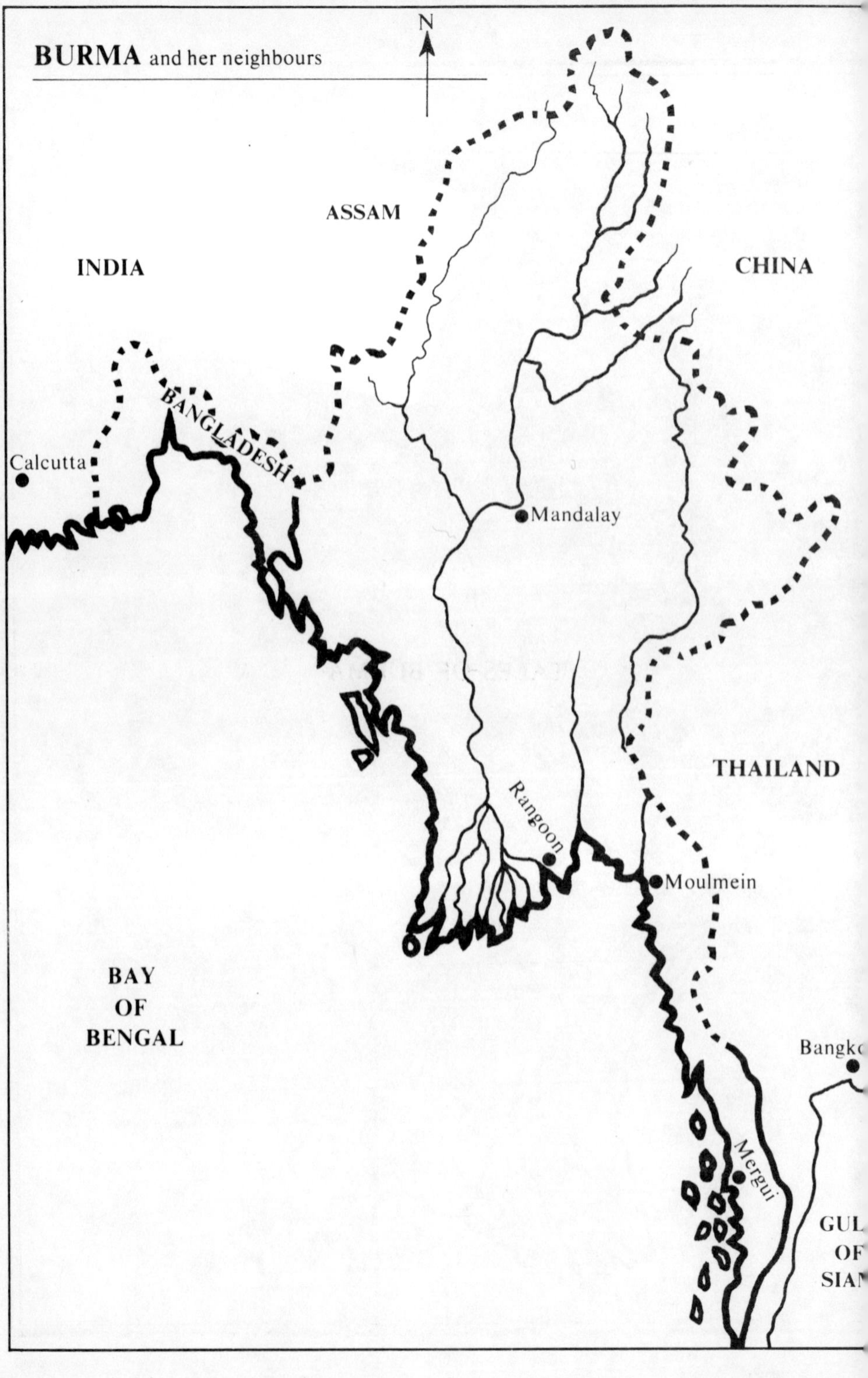
BURMA and her neighbours
N
ASSAM
INDIA
CHINA
BANGLADESH
Calcutta
Mandalay
THAILAND
Rangoon
Moulmein
BAY
OF
BENGAL
Bangk
Mergui
GUL
OF
SIA

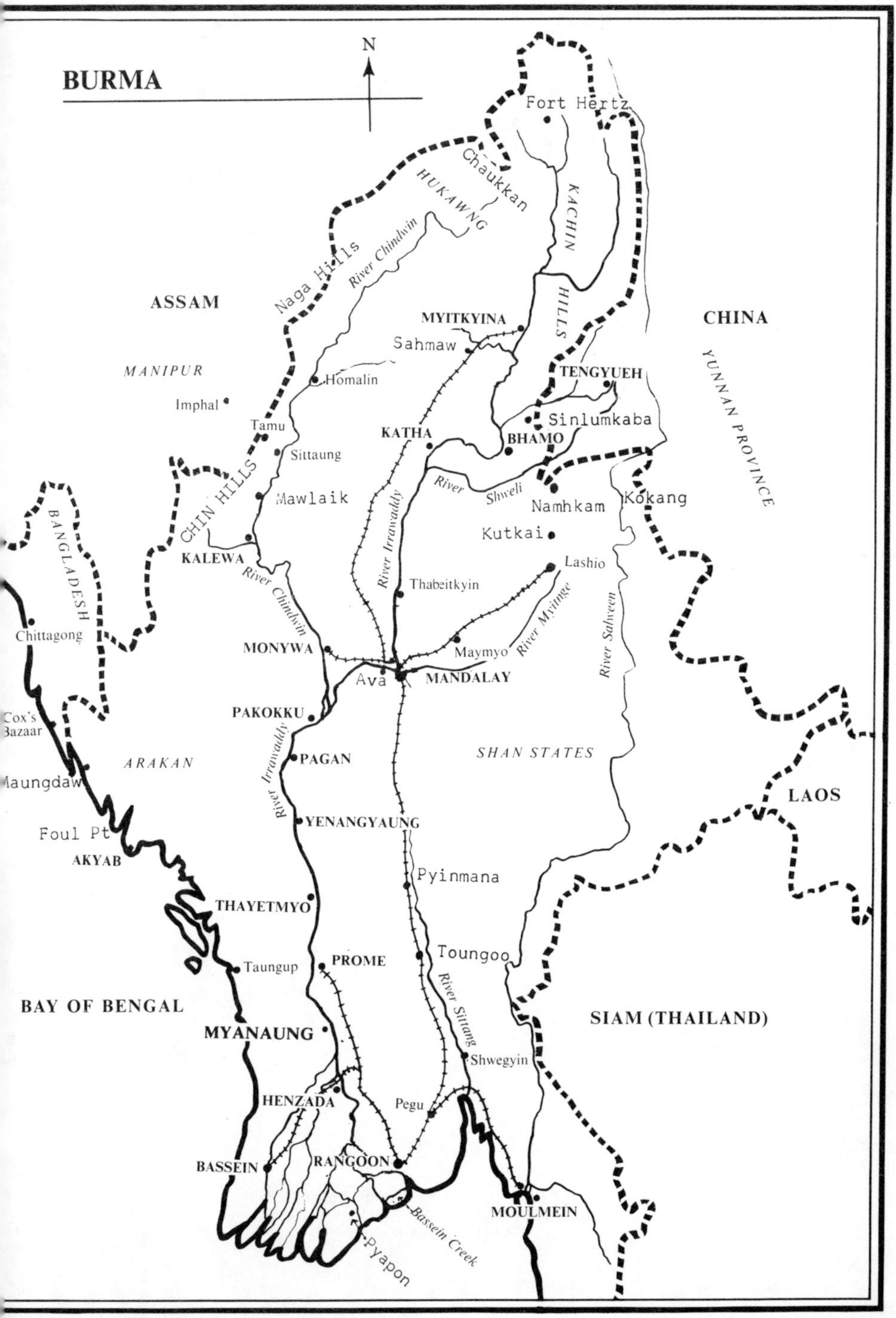
BURMA
N
ASSAM
MANIPUR
Imphal
CHINA
YUNNAN PROVINCE
Fort Hertz
Chaukkan
HUKAWNG
KACHIN
HILLS
Naga Hills
River Chindwin
MYITKYINA
Sahmaw
Homalin
TENGYUEH
Sinlumkaba
Tamu
Sittaung
KATHA
BHAMO
River
Shweli
Namhkam
Kokang
Mawlaik
CHIN HILLS
BANGLADESH
Kutkai
KALEWA
River Chindwin
Lashio
Thabeitkyin
River Irrawaddy
River Myitnge
River Salween
Chittagong
MONYWA
Maymyo
Ava
MANDALAY
Cox's Bazaar
PAKOKKU
ARAKAN
PAGAN
SHAN STATES
Maungdaw
River Irrawaddy
LAOS
YENANGYAUNG
Foul Pt
AKYAB
Pyinmana
THAYETMYO
Toungoo
Taungup
PROME
River Sittang
BAY OF BENGAL
SIAM (THAILAND)
MYANAUNG
Shwegyin
HENZADA
Pegu
BASSEIN
RANGOON
MOULMEIN
Bassein Creek
Pyapon

Published by JAMES PATON of PAISLEY
18 Gordon Street
PAISLEY PA1 1XB

First Published 1981

ISBN No. 0 9506061 38

Printed in Great Britain by James Paton Limited
at Gazette Office, 18 Gordon Street
PAISLEY PA1 1XB

Last splendour of the British days in Burma. The Governor leaving the King's palace in Mandalay after a durbar in 1940. The palace was destroyed by action during the Japanese war.

Books by the authors

Harold Braund

DISTINCTLY I REMEMBER
CALLING TO MIND

Alister McCrae & Alan Prentice

IRRAWADDY FLOTILLA

Hamish Mackay

A HISTORY OF THE 4th GURKHA RIFLES
1938-1948

HISTORY OF THE 7th GURKHA RIFLES

Noel Stevenson

THE HILL PEOPLES OF BURMA

ECONOMICS OF THE CENTRAL CHIN TRIBES

Tales of Burma

Compiled and Introduced
and with Biographies
by Alister McCrae

HAROLD BRAUND

RITCHIE GARDINER

CHRISTOPHER LORIMER

ALISTER MCCRAE

HAMISH MACKAY

HUGH NISBET

ALAN PRENTICE

NOEL STEVENSON

"TAWTHA"

A'po gyi oh ka kone gon
M'they ba nai ohn
Nauk hnit ka T'zaungmon pwè
Kyi ba ohn

Don't die yet
Bent-backed old man
Wait until next year
And see again
The Tazaungmon Festival

Proverbial Burmese verse

CONTENTS

GLOSSARY

Tale		
One	*Hpoongyi*	Buddhist monk
	Boh	Warrior, Captain
	Myo-ok	Magistrate
	dah	sword
	hypoongyi-chaung	monastery
	awza	influence, standing
	putsoe	man's silk skirt
	gaung-baung	man's silk headdress
	thakin	master
Three	*durwan*	watchman
Six	*hpoongyi-chaung*	monastery
	Sayadaw	Abbott
	hpoongyi-byan	ceremonial funeral
	lonedwin	dug-out long boat
	jeel	lake, or inundation of water
	Sawbwa	Ruler of a Shan State
	eingyi	Burmese jacket
	longyi	man's skirt
	lugale	servant (lit. small man)
	shey-ney	pleader
	putsoe	man's silk skirt
Eight	*Duwa*	Chief
	shingbwi	a palmate leaf
	chingkhyen	split bamboo flooring
	pachyet	long woven strip of cloth
	sharaw	tiger
	jihad	holy war
Nine	*oozie*	elephant rider
	Thakin	Master
	lugale	servant
Eleven	*Myosa*	minor Sawbwa of Shan sub-state
	yamen	palace
	Nampan Du	Flower Chief, nickname for Noel Stevenson
	Hpawngseng Du	Chief of Hpawngseng Tract

INTRODUCTION

The scenes for this collection of short stories are set on the rivers, the mountains and frontiers of Burma, and in the paddy fields and teak forests. They range in subject from rebellion in 1885 to the victory of the Fourteenth Army over the Japanese invader sixty years later.

Only one, Noel Stevenson's *A Back Door to Authority,* has appeared before, in Blackwood's Magazine; but all are written in the same vein of personal experience by men who lived and worked in Burma before the war of 1941-45. With the exception of one who wrote of 1885 and is long since dead, the authors all served in that war in the Armies of India and Burma.

For those who returned to their civilian occupations in Burma in 1946, hopeful and eager to restore life to a devastated economy, there was little time left. Burma achieved her Independence in 1948 and the British melted from the scene.

The "guest" authors, with the same one exception, are all my friends of long standing with whom bonds of being "old Burma hands" remain unbroken. I hope that my biographical notes of them will add to the interest of reading their tales of that fascinating and now little known country.

ONE

THE TWO HPOONGYIS

A Tale of the Pegu Rebellion 1885/86

by Hugh Nisbet

When General Prendergast took up his army to Mandalay in December 1885 he left Lower Burmah more or less denuded of troops; knowing this a rebellion was started in the Pegu District by two *hpoongyis* of the villages of Mawachaung and Kyaukelat on the Sittang River, with the idea of taking Rangoon after sacking Pegu.

Some two thousand men from the villages south of Toungoo to Kyassoo on the sea were enrolled under *Bohs*. Several *Myo-oks* were also sympathetic and arms were secured, first from Siam and later by attacking isolated police posts, and killing the men. In one case the *hpoongyis'* followers burnt a police post, Kaywa, with the policemen in it and committed other atrocities in the villages.

The Deputy Commissioner Weideman of Shwegyin wired for help to Rangoon and Symes, who was then Chief Secretary and a most able administrator, sensed danger and dispatched fifty of the Royal Scots Fusiliers to that place; and this was so quietly done that the rebels did not hear of their arrival.

When the rebels attacked Shwegyin one night, several hundred strong, they got such a reception that over forty were killed and about two hundred taken prisoners. This happened about the middle of December 1885.

Lower down the Sittang River the whole country was in the hands of the rebels. Pegu was in a state of seige and the Government would not allow any Europeans to go out into the district. Colonel Street and Colonel Strover, the Commissioners, were out with every available civil and military policeman and also De Courcy Ireland, the Inspector General of Police, and these officers were having constant skirmishes with rebels. The Bombay Burmah Trading Corporation had several hundred rafts of teak timber floating down the Sittang River; each raft carried four men and it was reported to Government that these men had all joined the *hpoongyis* men. When S. G. Jones, the

Corporation's Manager in Rangoon, heard of this he immediately arranged for me to go up and find out the truth, and also if possible save the timber, some 10,000/15,000 logs, from going out to sea. I was told to pick my best friend to assist me.

I got my orders at 6 p.m. on a Saturday at Kemmendine House in Rangoon and telephoned to our sawmill at Dallah to say I was coming over. In those days our fellows at Dallah used to have weekend parties of men from Rangoon and sometimes as many as sixteen sat down to dinner on a Saturday night. The firm were at that time engaging new men for forest operations in Upper Burmah and some six or eight had come from India to be interviewed by our chiefs, so there was a good crowd there when I got to Dallah about 7.30 p.m. I had fixed on B. B. Deane with whom I had worked for many years, and when I suggested his coming with me he jumped at the chance. So we arranged for the *Pifla,* one of our small launches, to leave for Tawa at the Pegu Lock Gates the next day, we ourselves going by train on Sunday morning to Pegu. Being late on Saturday we had little chance of getting stores together, but our office arranged to send us some later by rail.*

Sunday morning saw us off to Pegu and on arrival there the Commissioners informed us that they would not be responsible for our lives if we went into the district. However, we decided to go on. Deane went with our kit in carts and a police guard to the lock gates by road, and I by train to Tawa. He arrived at Tawa shortly after I did, and that evening our launch from Dallah turned up. Luckily we had secured some tinned foods in the Pegu bazaar, so we got the launch into the Pegu Canal that night, to make an early start the next morning.

The following afternoon we arrived at Minywa where we found Moultrie, Extra Assistant Commissioner, and about twelve Military Policemen. They had stockaded the dak bungalow and were expecting an attack from rebels that very evening. He begged us to stop the night as our extra pair of rifles would come in useful if the rebels attacked. This we did. All night long scouts came in to report that rebels were coming, but they did not come and we heard afterwards that Colonel Street with his men had given them a dressing down that afternoon.

The next day we pushed on through the canal and arrived in the afternoon at Waw. Much to our surprise we saw a European officer and some twenty-five policemen drawn up on the bank. Deane and I, feeling so glad to see a white man, came up the

*See map on page 17.

bank, I holding two bottles of beer and he with a whisky bottle and two sodas. We were saluted by the policemen and the officer came forward and gave us full reports of the rebels and what had happened, thinking, as he said afterwards, that one of us was at least a Commissioner! He turned out to be Pockett of the Burmah Police. When he had dismissed his men he was very glad to put some beer into him as he had been "out on the *dah*" for several days.

Saying goodbye to him later, we pushed on for Myitkyo, the head of the Pegu Canal. At Abaya, however, we discovered that the bund had been cut by rebels and that we could not get to Myitkyo by canal but would have to go down to the Sittang River through the Abaya Creek. It was just a chance that we might get through as the tide was coming up, so we risked it. We managed to do so, though we got aground at one place where there were about fifteen Burmans standing in the khinegrass. We asked them if they would help to push off the launch and this they did, and we left after giving them five rupees for their help. These men, we found afterwards, were rebels and they had hidden their guns in the khinegrass and come to our help. Why they did not attack us has always remained a mystery to me.

At the mouth of the Abaya Creek we came to a deserted village and decided to tie up for the night. In the distance we saw many villages burning on both sides of the river but no sign of anyone about. Just before dusk we went into the deserted village, Alokekoon, and noticed a lot of straw lying about. I was walking over it when I felt something under my feet. Thinking it might be a pig we removed the straw to find a Burman who told us he was the headman of the village, that they had been attacked by rebels and everything taken away that they could lay their hands on, and through fear he had hidden himself under the straw. He was overjoyed at seeing us and promised to give us all the help possible.

The headman turned out to be a splendid fellow and besides helping us to salve rafts, brought in every day vegetables etc. for which we were very thankful. He appeared to know all about our raftsmen and told us that when the rebellion started all the raftsmen left their rafts and returned to Toungoo as they were afraid of the rebels; it was quite untrue that any of our men had joined the *hpoongyis'* men. He told us also of several *Myo-oks* and other officials who, pretending to be loyal, joined the rebellion and gave the rebels information; also that these two *hpoongyis* were clever fellows and had some of the most fearless men as their lieutenants, that for two or three months meetings had been going on at their *hpoongyi-kyaungs* on moonlight nights, that they picked out the brave men in this way: the hpoongyi held a *dah* in his hand and made every man walk with his head down showing the back of his neck, the *hpoongyi* would bring the *dah* down sharply within a few inches of the man's neck and if he did not flinch he was made a *Boh*. This made all the young bloods eager to be chosen and in this way they got some fine recruits.

I visited Kyaukelat during my stay and found the *hpoongyi-kyaung* on top of a steep hillock about 3/400 feet up. There was only one steep path to the top, and all around the other sides of the hill sharpened bamboo spikes had been stuck into the ground in the grass so that anyone going up except by the steep path would get spiked. I remember thinking that the place could have been held by a few men, it was such a natural fortress. One of the rebels who had surrendered took us over the place secretly, as we might have been attacked if it was known that we were going there.

With the help of the headman we started the salving of the teak rafts. Luckily we had come up just in time, the neap tides were on and so the timber did not float out to sea so quickly. After salving all rafts below Alokekoon we pushed on to Myitkyo, salving rafts on the way, tying up at a village every night. When we came to a village the villagers returned from the jungle and helped us, and when we left they and their families left again and hid every night in the elephant grass. It took several days to get to Myitkyo. On arriving there we saw that the lock gates had been burnt by the rebels and were told by the villagers who came back from hiding that the rebels had come there a few days before to get recruits and found only an old man and woman in the village. They were so enraged that they took these two old people, tied straw round them, poured kerosene oil on the straw and after tying up one on each side of the lock gates, set fire to them and the lock gates, which of course we found burned out.

Whilst patrolling and picking up rafts, for two or three nights we had tied up alongside of us two Naval launches under Lt. Warren of the H.M.S. *Woodlark*. With them Deane and I foregathered and were very glad to have them with us. These launches had been sent up by Government to help the local authorities.

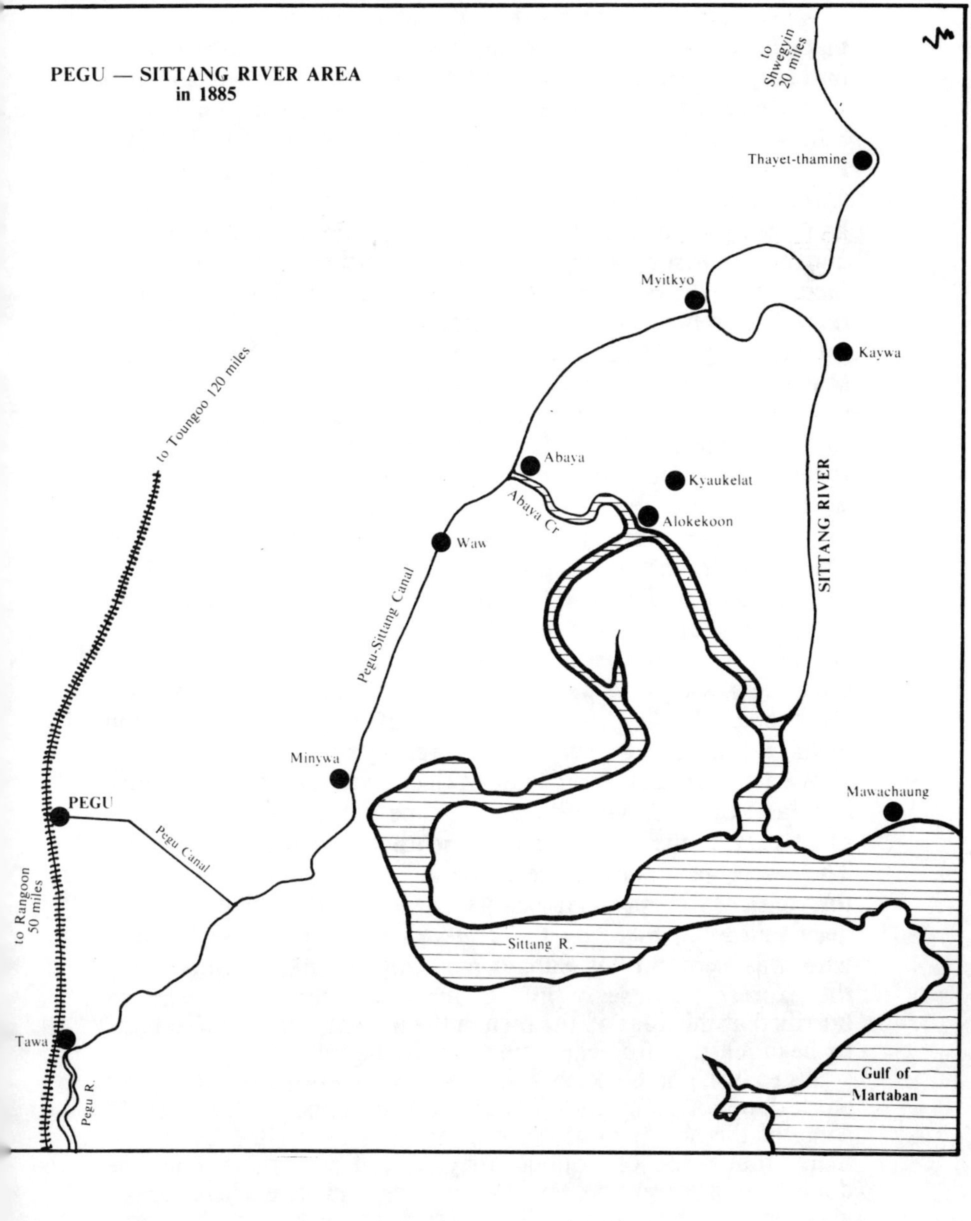
PEGU — SITTANG RIVER AREA
in 1885
to Shwegyin 20 miles
Thayet-thamine
Myitkyo
Kaywa
to Toungoo 120 miles
Abaya
Kyaukelat
Abaya Cr
Alokekoon
Waw
SITTANG RIVER
Pegu-Sittang Canal
Minywa
PEGU
Mawachaung
Pegu Canal
to Rangoon 50 miles
Sittang R.
Tawa
Pegu R.
Gulf of
Martaban

After having salved all the rafts at Myitkyo and below, we made for Shwegyin to get some provisions, as we had been living on curry and rice, some erbswurst soup and country vegetables with a chicken or fish whenever we could get them. We reached Shwegyin on New Year's Eve 1886, and found a Captain of the Royal Scots Fusiliers in command of fifty of his Regiment at the Circuit House. All the women and children of the local officials had been placed in two houses and guarded by military police, and many prisoners were in jail. This officer asked us to join them at their Mess to see the New Year in, but we had to regretfully refuse; we were after food and had to get back to our rafts that night. He told us how lucky it had been that they were sent by Symes to Shwegyin just in time, otherwise the place would have been sacked by the rebels with all the horrors known to the Burmese in these days. As it was, the Fusiliers gave the rebels such a hot reception when they did attack that over forty were killed and some two hundred taken prisoners.

A few days more, just as our work was done, we received urgent orders from Rangoon through Lt. Napier, the officer commanding at Thayet-Thamine, to return to Rangoon and not to bother about the timber. The Company had sent up an old Burman, Ko Oung Hla, one of our most trusted men, to look after the work as he was a man who had great *awza* amongst the people. We had had three weeks of really roughing it, and whilst we were extremely fit, we were glad to return.

We left our launch *Pifla* at Myitkyo and got on to a native boat and came down the canal. Deane and I rowed the boat a great part of the way to Tawa and thence railed to Rangoon. They were very glad to see us back, as the Company had lost four of their European Assistants on the Chindwin River, having been murdered there by the *Thandawzin*, a Burmese General who was sent up by Supayalat, King Thebaw's Queen, for the express purpose of killing our men. Our chiefs were so horrified at this that all the men in the jungles were ordered back to headquarters for fear others would be killed.

When we got back to Rangoon and reported all the good work done for us by the villagers, salving timber, and especially some of the headmen of the villages, thus saving the Company many thousands of pounds, they agreed something must be done to commemorate this. At my suggestion, each headman was sent a *putsoe* and each villager a *gaung-baung*. For some years after in that district I was referred to by the villagers as the *gaung-baung* and the *putsoe thakin*.

I went home on leave in March 1886, and on returning to Rangoon in November of the same year, whilst in office, a woman and two children turned up with the pitiable tale that her husband, the headman of Alokekoon village, who had been the best helper we had, had been convicted on false evidence by the Sessions Judge at Pegu for having harboured rebels. Jones, my chief, immediately got the Company's lawyers, Messrs. Gilbanks and Sumners, on to it, and on appeal we succeeded in getting the old fellow off, for we were able to prove that he had nothing to do with the rebels. With some rupees to rebuild his house, he and his wife and children went off happily.

By the beginning of the New Year the authorities had succeeded in crushing the rebellion, some hundreds of rebels had been killed and many more sentenced to transportation for life. As regards the two *hpoongyis*, the Kyaukelat was killed in one of the skirmishes with the police, but the Mawachaung *hpoongyi* went across the border into Karenni. I heard of him when I was with Colonel Sartorious' southern column on the expedition to Karenni in 1888, but I do not think that he was ever caught.

HUGH NISBET

I never knew Hugh Nisbet. His service in Burma spanned the years 1879 to 1914; thereafter he lived in retirement in England until his death in 1943. But his story, by a long way the first of these tales to be written, has been in my possession in a collection of Burma memoirs for many years.

For some notes on Nisbet's Burma service I am indebted to Peter Pointon, historian of the Bombay Burmah Trading Corporation (BBTCL) and a Forest Manager in Burma and Siam until his retiral in 1950. At the time of the Pegu rebellion, immediately before the British annexation of Upper Burma in January 1886, BBTCL held leases for the extraction of teak in British Lower Burma and also in the Upper Burma forests of the Burmese kings. They were, and continued to be, the largest of the British timber companies in Burma.

When Hugh Nisbet went out to Burma in 1879 straight from school in England to join BBTCL he was only seventeen, an unusually young age to begin Eastern service; but his father was in Rangoon practising as a doctor, having earlier served for many years in India and Burma in the Indian Medical Service. The experience of the still young Hugh during the Pegu rebellion was but a beginning to several adventurous years, for he was later temporarily enlisted as a special Inspector of Police during the troubled period which followed the annexation. In the expedition to Karenni with Colonel Sartorious, to quote but one example, the objective was to recapture stolen elephants. Consider the finding of even such large animals in dense jungle and then the problem of rounding them up.

The tale of the two hpoongyis has been retold just as Hugh Nisbet wrote it, close on a hundred years ago.

Note: *Burma* was spelt with an *h*, thus *Burmah*, up to around the turn of the century, when the *h* gradually disappeared.

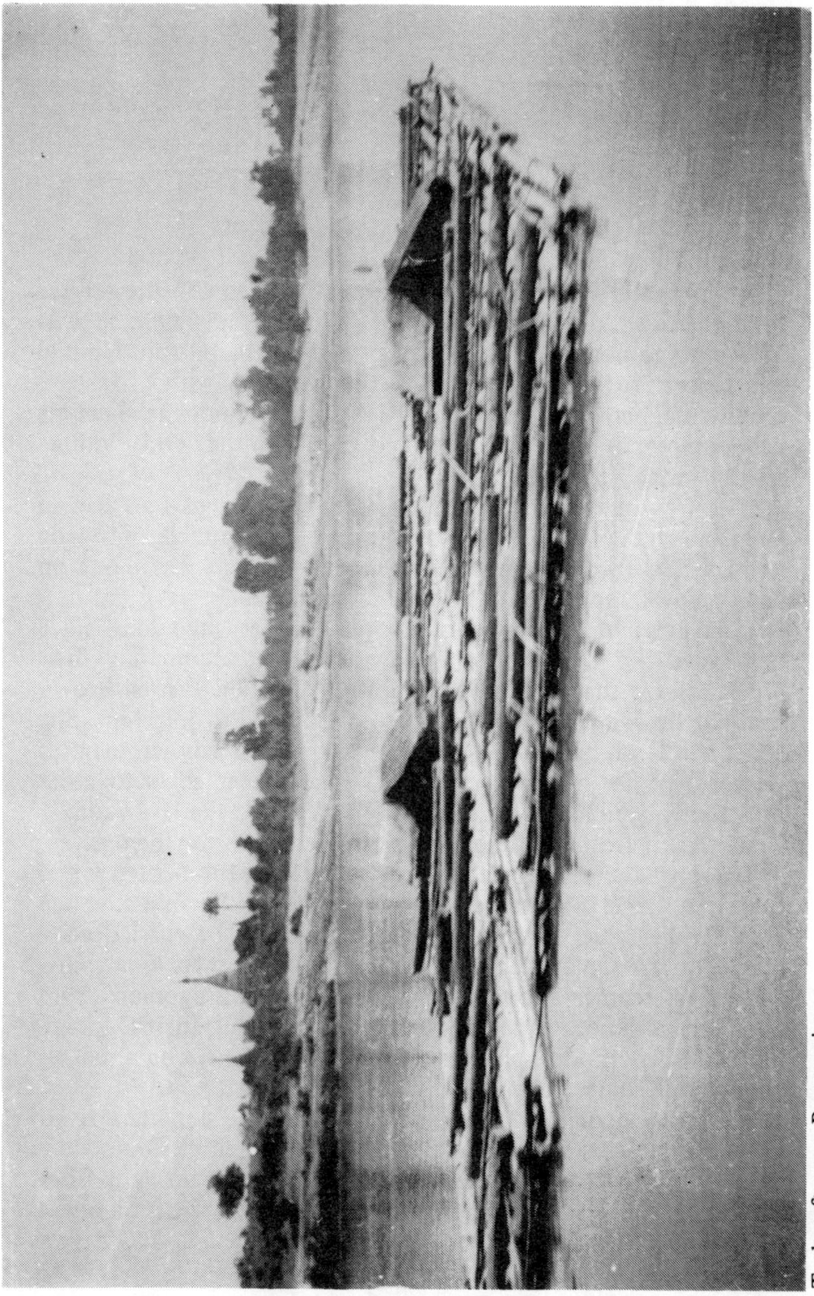

Teak raft on a Burma river.

TWO

CAPTAIN'S WIFE

by Alister McCrae

Captain Frank Powell-Brown had been ten years in the service of the Irrawaddy Flotilla Company in Burma when he was appointed to command the steamer *Ava* on the oil run. He had left the sea for the river in 1898, at the age of 26, with a Master's Certificate, had soon passed for River Master and was given his first command. He was destined to stay with the "Old Flotilla" for 28 years.

Ava was one of a number of side paddlers of 250 feet in length, built specially for oil towage. She was capable of towing two oil flats (tank barges) of 1000 tons capacity each, one on each side of the ship at the paddle sponsons.

Loneliness in command of an oil steamer had long since persuaded the Company to allow wives to accompany their husbands on the oil run and in 1908 Captain Powell-Brown brought his wife out to Burma from England to join him. She spent a year on board *Ava* and being a talented lady wrote notes on some of her experiences. Later she collected these together and in 1911 published a little book "A Year on the Irrawaddy". The extracts from this book which follow speak for themselves.

There was one other European on the *Ava,* the Scotch Chief Engineer. Lack of suitable accommodation in the ship was one reason why Chief Engineers' wives could not be carried also; and the *Ava* Chief was resigned to lead his own lonely life. Crews on steamer and flats were otherwise Chittagonians from East Bengal, fine watermen and intensely loyal to their Captain, but with whom discipline demanded that there could be no meaningful social contact.

So it was a lonely life on the oil run. When the steamer arrived up at the oilfields in Central Burma with flats either completely empty or with a deck load of oil well material brought from Rangoon for the fields, two laden oil flats were ready for a quick turnround and departure down river. At Rangoon no more than two days for bunkering was the order and off again up river with

Paddle Steamer ‘Ava’, Captain Powell-Brown’s command on the oil run.

another pair of empty flats. On the round trip of ten to twelve days the night stops were at anchor in mid-stream.

The Burma climate was warming up late in the month of February, 1908 — progressively the heat increases until the rains break in May — when Mrs Powell-Brown arrived in Rangoon. She opens her account by describing how her husband took her by launch to join *Ava* at the oil anchorage at the Hastings, beyond the Rangoon harbour limits.

"How fortunate we were to get a launch instead of having to undertake a rather perilous crossing in a sampan. The tide is running out like a mill race and had we been in a sampan and had we fouled a buoy or a ship's cable this would never have been written; so broad and deep is the river, so swift and strong the current, there is little chance of rescue for anyone capsized in the stream. In fact, few Europeans patronise a sampan when any other craft is available.

"We arrive safely on board. After dinner we go forward to enjoy the breeze and escape from the mosquitoes in the saloon. Now the darkness has fallen and the night is pleasantly cool. The Skipper points out to me the lights of Rangoon harbour, the anchored deep-sea ships of many nationalities; he says nearly all will be loading rice and most will belong to the great British India Company. They lie in a long parallel line down the harbour, tugging at the buoys to which they swing. Burma is by far the greatest exporter of rice in the world.

"The night is full of sound; the water lapping on our bows, the clank of the chain as the ship swings to the breeze, occasional trumpeting of elephants in the timber yard on the Rangoon shore and shrill hootings from bustling little steam launches threading their way across the harbour. The creaking of a sampan grows nearer and nearer, then the plash of oars and bumping and grating at the foot of the steamer's ladder followed by voluble chatter in a strange language as a returning *kalassi* (lascar seaman)* haggles over the fare with the sampan-wallah.

"The sound of a bugle comes faintly across the water from a homeward bound Bibby liner laden with passengers escaping the approaching hot weather; she is awaiting the tide below the Hastings and will soon be off. Some of the passengers are British or American tourists returning after a pleasant cold weather holiday; but most — we had seen them embarking — are jaded

*All the nautical words used are in Hindustani

"Anglo-Indian wrecks" with pallid faces, the women white of hue, the men ashen grey. Two passengers had been carried aboard too ill to walk; and one of them, we heard later, gave up the struggle and was "disembarked" in a weighted sack in the Red Sea.

"Then comes a far off searchlight from down stream, flickering across the sky. Nearer and nearer it comes and then a deep-toned boom, sounding at intervals, heralds the arrival of a Flotilla Company mail steamer from Mandalay. She is huge compared to *Ava,* 326 feet in length and the beam is some 150 feet with flats. She punches her way past against the last of the ebb tide and in to the Company's jetties within the harbour. Says the Skipper 'Some poor devil still hard at work. Let's turn in'."

Mrs Powell-Brown begins another description of her year on the Irrawaddy in a style reminiscent of Robert Louis Stevenson.

"Life on an oil steamer is a solitary existence. Government regulations prohibit us from lying alongside any landing stage or ghat. It is a tedious matter to go ashore or visit other vessels; the strong current makes the use of our heavy cutter difficult. In Rangoon we cannot enter the harbour limits and are anchored two miles away from the city.

"All this goes to explain that the Skipper and I are almost wholly dependent on each other for society. We seldom come into close contact with Burmese people, or any people apart from those on the ship, and have few opportunities of visiting towns, pagodas and lovely bits of scenery we see along the banks. So I make no attempt to write of the country and its people. I have learnt to look at everything from the navigator's point of view. I know the awkward places in the river, the eccentricities of the crew, the trials of the Commander and the various "tempers" of different vessels".

She takes us on a typical voyage of the oil steamer from Rangoon to the oilfields of the Burmah Oil Company at Yenangyaung; and back to deliver the laden oil flats to the Rangoon refineries at Syriam. So we return to the anchorage at the Hastings. It is dawn and as soon as there is sufficient light the first of the empty flats for *Ava* is dropped down from the buoy ahead to be made fast to the ship. The deck *Serang* is in charge; he is the Captain's man, selected by him, for there is no Mate. The Company sign on the *Serang* only and he brings with him the permitted number of men, his *kalassies* and two *secunnies* (helmsmen). All are Chittagonians and it is likely that most will be related to the *Serang* and completely obedient to him. The reason for the latter will already be obvious.

"With much shouting from the *Serang* the huge iron hulk of the flat, as long as the vessel herself, is hove into position and made fast for towing. Meanwhile the second flat appears. A Company's tug, looking uncommonly like a frail little woman leading home a burly drunken husband, comes panting up from Syriam with our other flat.

"At length all is ready for departure, but no! The saloon boy rushes up to say that the butler has not yet arrived back on board with the stores. The Skipper receives this calmly; he has half an hour to spare. But the time passes on; he becomes fidgety; he becomes annoyed; he becomes exasperated; he becomes desperate. He alternates between the whistle lanyard and the telescope. If that rascally member of the Madrassi race (saloon staffs were mostly Madrassis) does not come soon, very soon, he has either to leave Rangoon with no food on board or to miss the tide at the Bassein Creek and so lose a day. He paces up and down the for'ard deck; again he drags at the whistle lanyard; again he raises the telescope and scans the jetties and the river. Is he there? Yes, at last he comes to view in a distant sampan seated imperturbably nursing a stack of cabbages, with joints of meat, tins of milk, bottles of soda water and various other provisions piled in confusion around him. The sampan crawls across the river and eventually reaches the ship.

" 'Stand by!' roars the skipper. He has no time to talk to the delinquent now and no doubt the wily one knew this. 'Better to be a lot than a little late' thinks he, and the Captain's anger has time to cool off before the inevitable interview takes place.

"The windlass has already begun to heave in the anchor, the *secunnie* is at the wheel and the *puriwalla* (Captain's factotum) at the telegraph. Two men are at the wheel of each flat watching and waiting for orders. 'Easy ahead' says the Skipper. The anchor is a-weigh and the huge paddle wheels turn slowly and begin to churn up the water. 'Half speed' rings out and the engines respond; then as the anchor is heaved aboard 'full speed' and away we go leaving a yellow wake of water behind as we turn and swing into the channel, heading down river for the Bassein Creek."

The Bassein Creek is some fifteen miles from the anchorage. The open sea is visible to the south at the creek entrance; at the other end, forty miles away, is the main Irrawaddy estuary, known as China Bakir. The creek itself is a navigator's nightmare. The tide flows in at either end and as a natural consequence runs out the same way. Entry by steamer had to be timed to a nicety and passage through the narrow and tortuous first twenty miles made within prescribed time limits. The creek then widens after passing a tiny village which marks the half way and the meeting of the tides. Passing of other steamers coming in from the China Bakir end was then possible and their entry had to be timed accordingly. The consequences of delays from grounding or other causes need no explanation. That there were few speaks for the skills of the steamer Captains.

The Skipper's wife never ceased to be anxious for him as he took his ship through this creek, his concentration never relaxing for a moment in the five hour passage.

"He sits at a table in front of the wheel and by a movement of his hands directs the helmsman. *'Dina nay'* he says ('not to starboard') and *'dina nay'* repeats the *secunnie,* steadying the steamer on her course. Then there is a sharp bend ahead. The wheel is put hard over but she does not answer her helm and a collision with the bank seems imminent. Up springs the Skipper and with circling arms shouts to the flats' helmsmen; their rudders are manhandled over with haste but she changes course just a moment too late. 'Stop her! Back her easy' he calls calmly to the *puriwalla*. We bump gently against the bank and scratch along tearing at bushes — but there is no damage to steamer or flats.

"An old Burman in a canoe has a narrow escape. He and his boat are washed up on the bank and left stranded in the mud. He clings to the trees with his hands and to the boat with his feet; and when the danger is past smiles and assures us with a wave that there is no harm done.

"At last we reach the China Bakir, with the open sea on our left hand and the wide arm of the river on our right. The Skipper means to run late tonight and has given orders that there are to be no lights on the upper deck after nightfall; he will navigate in the broad lower waters without the searchlight. We take advantage of the last of the daylight to have an early dinner and as darkness falls around 6 p.m. he settles down to a six hour watch. He was at work at 4 a.m. and means to run until midnight; a day's work of twenty hours. As for me, I try to keep awake and bear him company, but the night is cold and weariness overcomes me. I retire, ready for another early start tomorrow. We shall be anchoring only for a few hours and be off again before daybreak. Thus we shall reach Myanaung on the second night and have put behind us 250 miles of our run of 450 miles to the oilfields at Yenangyaung."

Only once in her book does Mrs Powell-Brown mention the Chief Engineer. This was obviously not due to any antagonism between deck and engine room; far from it, for she writes in sympathetic terms of their shipmate.

"At Prome, where we anchor for the third night, we receive the home mail which has been sent up by train from Rangoon. One pilot is sent ashore there and the next, with the letters in his charge, is brought off. We anxiously watch the boat nearing the ship; and the *puriwalla,* who knows that haste is expedient, stands waiting on the flat. He seizes the packet before anything else is handed out of the boat and runs with it to the Skipper who is ready, knife in hand, to cut the string. He stands by while the letters and papers are sorted and then runs along with a goodly pile to the Chief Engineer. The arrival of the mail is a very big event to him because his wife and the child he has never yet seen are in Scotland and the weekly mail is all the solace *he* gets out of married life for five long years."

Pilotage played an important part in ensuring safe passage for the Irrawaddy river steamers, particularly in the low water season. The first pilot for the *Ava* had come aboard at Myanaung where, with the delta left behind, the course of the river was constantly changing and the local knowledge of the pilots was invaluable. The second pilot beat started at Prome and there were three more beats before reaching Yenangyaung on the fifth day. Some of the pilots were Chittagonians, men from ships who had settled in villages at one or other end of a beat, others local Burmese villagers who had adapted to a Mark Twain existence. All were competent or they were soon paid off. The Pilot Master was a senior Captain who looked after that. He had pilots stationed on no less than fifteen beats from Myanaung to Bhamo, the farthest north point to which steamers navigated, a thousand miles from Rangoon. And in the low water season small steam buoying launches under his control marked the channels; all were provided by the Company. They had a near monopoly of the river trade.

The highlights of the last two days on the upwards trip of *Ava* were the sunsets of the central plain of Burma, vividly described by the Captain's wife.

"When the sun sinks below the horizon there is a rapid change from day to night, so sudden and unexpected that it leaves one almost breathless. There is no twilight as in England, no gloaming, no quiet restful time between daylight and darkness. Rapidly, as in the transformation scene in a pantomime, the colours change, mingle, fade and disappear into liquid blackness. One moment there is sunlight, glaring and merciless, the river a brazen, blinding mass of molten metal; gold-topped pagodas sheeted in flame; dazzling white spires and vivid foliage hazy and pulsing in an overwhelming superfluity of light. Another moment and the hurtful glare, the keen spiky radiance, have gone. All is now diffused in a rosy glow, the water is pink, the thatch on the riverside houses is flushed with soft colour, the sky flecked with crimson. Land and water and sky are bathed in a purple flood in which there is every shade from heliotrope to violet, from mauve to the richest blue. Colour succeeds colour until at last the river flows down in an indigo stream, a reflection of the darkening sky overhead; night has come.

"Tonight there is no moon. Arched overhead is velvety darkness, pricked out with stars. There is the Southern Cross, shining out on our port quarter; and the familiar "home" stars are there too. I am seated on deck in the fore end of the vessel watching the scene. The helmsman, with the marvellous eyesight of his race, is guiding his course by the black outlines of the distant bank, but there are shoals and buoyed channels ahead and the Skipper's order goes forth *'Burra batti chellao'* ('on with the big light') and a sudden gleam spurts out from the searchlight in the bows. The Skipper goes to the searchlight motor, manipulates the handle and the light travels round, a tongue of fire, licking the edges of the land. It falls on a little fleet of Burmese country boats anchored for mutual protection against dacoits; and the sleeping men start up in consternation. Then the light passes on.

"Our searchlight has the power of Midas; when it touches on an already golden pagoda the effect is so dazzling that one almost expects sparks to fly. Grim black shapes shine out as green hills crowned with delicate white pagodas. Then the light sinks and sweeps the surface of the water as the Skipper switches it from side to side until it catches a distant sandbank and then keeps it there until we are safely by. Further ahead there are bamboo buoys marking off dangerous shallows and submerged rocks.

"As we approach the buoys the cries of the leadsmen from the bows of the flats on each side become more rapid and insistent. The droning *'teen bahm mila nai'* ('not getting three fathoms') gives place to *'sari do bahm'* ('two and a half fathoms') then *'sari ek bahm'* ('one and a half') in quick succession. We get safely through apart from one little bump. It is a relief to be out in the open water once more and going full speed upstream.

"We perceive a moving gleam ahead, a shadowy wave of light rolling along the landscape. It grows and intensifies until one realises at last that it is the searchlight of an overtaking steamer. 'Mail Boat' says the Skipper as he directs our searchlight over the starboard bow; that of the mail steamer is playing about like a serpent's tongue, occasionally glinting on our stanchions, turning them into white hot luminous metal, dazzling to look upon. Then comes a long low blast of a whistle, much superior to ours in the depth of its tone and the *R.M.S. Ceylon* slowly passes us, electric lights twinkling from stem to stern. We can see the swinging *punkahs* and whirling fans in the saloon and the engineer's mess room. The butler and his white robed staff are running to and fro attending to the wants of the first class passengers. The open decks are crowded with Burmese, Indian and some Chinese passengers, their sleeping mats placed in long rows side by side and almost touching, for there will be close on three thousand persons on board. Here and there are yellow robed *hpoongyis,* and little children have gathered at the rails to look at us and exult over the faster speed of their vessel. Soon we are left rocking in her wash and watch her moving on ahead. She will run all night, with the relieving night Commander on board; but for us on the smaller vessel the day's work is done. An order from the Skipper and the paddles slow down to silence, the searchlight sweeps round for the last time then is darkened, leaving everything strangely dull and quiet. The Skipper strides forward, leans over the rail and speaks quietly to the *Serang* on the lower deck, then *'chore-do'* ('let go') he says and a rattle and splash follow his words as the anchor falls."

When the *Ava* and her empty flats arrived next day at Nyaunghla, the riverine port for the Yenangyaung oilfields, the routine was followed. The Burmese Agent came out by sampan as soon as they were anchored with orders for the placing of the flats and for the down trip. The steamer has to proceed some miles further up river to load groundnuts; the season's crop was in and the regular services could not cope with the demand for space. So the chance was not missed to fill up the otherwise empty holds and decks of the oil steamers. And it was good for the Skipper too, for he earned some extra commission on the freight. Mrs Powell-Brown continued her account.

"We spend the night alongside the bank where this great pile of groundnut bags is stacked. The Skipper decides how much he will take. He has already told the Nyaunghla Agent the draughts to which his oil flats are to be loaded, having seen the latest telegrams from Bhamo with the gauge reading of the river level.

"Next morning we return to Nyaunghla, pick up the two loaded oil flats which are ready for us and the downward journey commences. The groundnuts we are carrying are oily and the shells as dry as tinder, while the bags they are in have been baked in the sun until they are almost charred. It is a most inflammable cargo, to say nothing of the fact the we have about seven hundred tons of crude oil in each flat on either side of us. The skipper has given very special warnings about lights and smoking and is constantly impressing upon me 'in case of fire, run aft' because anyone getting into the water from the forward end would only be washed back into the paddle wheels. He explains that I must run aft because, should there be danger, he would let go the anchor, the ship would swing round to it with head upstream and the flats cut loose; the crew always have hatchets ready just in case.

"I confess that I feel a little nervous at times, but one soon gets used to these dangers. One would run much worse risks for the sake of living with one's husband on the river, with the alternative of enduring a lonely existence in the steamy heat of Rangoon.

"At this time of year, in the north east monsoon period, it is much hotter on the downward journey because we are travelling in the same direction as the breeze, what there is of it, and the deck cargo of bags prevent it reaching us from aft. The reverse will be the case when the south west monsoon comes, but that does not worry me much either.

"We anchor for the night long before dark because north of Prome there is a rock channel which we could not reach before nightfall. Next morning we come to this channel, enter serenely but are not quite quick enough taking the bend; the starboard flat sways into shoal water and shoves her nose down into the mud, while the ship forges ahead. The towing ropes squeak and groan as the extra strain falls on them and then snap with loud reports like pistol shots as the flat parts company with the steamer. '*Unda boat nungle chore do*' ('let go flat's anchor') roars the Skipper as the flat swings round with the current. The anchor holds but the stern strikes the rocky bank, buckling the heavy rudder. Of course, that is bad enough but it is a fortunate thing that the flat is not punctured as well. An hour's strenuous work then follows, not without its dangers too, picking up the flat again, passing new towing lines; and then we proceed, dropping down the channel stern first on our anchor and missing the outlying ledge of rock by practically nothing at all.

"We reach Prome at noon but our delay with the parted flat has given another oil steamer, the *Pekin*, a chance to catch us up. She arrives at the same time as we do and each Skipper tries to be first to pick up the waiting pilot, as there could be delay before another is roused from his home and comes down to the shore. As soon as we are turned round our boat is away, but the boat from *Pekin* has started too and a most exciting race takes place. The other crew reach the station flat first but in their haste crash into it and bungle over throwing the painter; so our men steal in and carry off the pilot triumphantly leaving the *Pekin* to wait for the next man. The Skipper is quite jubilant over his success and gives a tantalising hoot on the whistle as we get under way again. But there is a sequel to this.

"We anchor that night at the last of daylight. No point in running late as we have ample time next day to be down off the Bassein Creek for the tide on the day following. An hour later a steamer passes down; the Skipper recognises her. 'It's the *Pekin* — he must be going for tomorrow's tide. What's the man made of!' But there was a special reason for the haste as we find out when we reach Rangoon. The Chief Engineer of *Pekin* had a telegram at Prome saying that his wife was ill and he was in a fever of anxiety until they reached Rangoon. He got there just in time to be with her over a crisis and she made a good recovery. How he blessed his Captain.

"It is at moments like this, when one is reminded of sickness or death near at hand that a feeling of exile comes over one, a mad longing to escape, to struggle against the fetters that bind one to a foreign land, to do anything rather than live away from the dear home country. However, that passes and we are grateful for the recovery of the Chief's wife.

"Next evening as we pass Dedaye, last station on the now widening China Bakir, the Skipper looks out for orders which are chalked large on a huge blackboard and displayed on the station flat:—

Flat 86 — Syriam
Flat 112 — Hastings

"So to Rangoon the next day. As we near the Hastings we see a messenger on a nearby flat waiting to put off in a sampan and bring letters across to us. Mail from home to give us a welcome end to our voyage."

THREE

A BACK DOOR TO AUTHORITY

By Noel Stevenson

I was twenty-two at the time, and restless. Two years' rubber planting in the sticky heat of King Island in the Mergui Archipelago had turned my thoughts to the cool north of Burma, and in particular to a place called Khamti Long—the Golden Plain of botanist-explorer Kingdon Ward's romantic wanderings — which seemed to be a veritable paradise. I had no idea how I was going to get there, but as a start I decided to take a job on a sugar plantation a thousand miles north at Sahmaw, a couple of stations south of the railhead at Myitkyina and on the edge of the Kachin Hills, which stretch away to the borders of Yunnan and Tibet. It was a fateful move, for it brought me into contact with the Kachins, at that time still wild, feuding tribesmen, a large part of whose territory was unadministered. They came in hundreds to cut cane on the Sahmaw estate, and their bold airs and rumbustious cheerfulness soon captured my affection. Like the Gurkhas, they bind all who live among them with unbreakable bonds of trust and friendship.

Some months later, convalescing in Myitkyina after an attack of malaria, I decided to visit the hill eyries of my two Kachin henchmen, Magawng Gam and Jatawng La. Gam was the son of a rebel headman, La the heir of a patrician chief. Both lived on the borders of the unadministered Triangle between the two great arms of the Irrawaddy. They were as merry and tough a pair of scallywags as ever walked, and where they went I knew I need not hesitate to follow. I found, however, that there was a snag. The Kachin Hills were in the so-called Scheduled Areas. Strangers were not welcomed by the Administration. The district commissioner had flatly refused to let me wander about there on my own, Kachin-wise, on the grounds that it would be bad for the white man's image. I had argued in vain that Colonel Lewin, one of the most famous administrators of the Lushai Hills to the west, had first ventured in alone with nothing but a rucksack on his back.

I was burning with frustrated anger as I made my way back to the Circuit House, where I lodged, and not mollified when I found it strewn with boxes and baggage of all kinds through which I had difficulty in picking my way. In the midst of it all stood a tall, gaunt, monocled Englishman, and as I stumbled past him I noted his name on one of the boxes — Darcy Weatherbe. It rang a bell. A year before, the Burma papers had been full of the story of an explorer of that name who had been captured on his way overland from Peking and held to ransom by Chinese bandits, from whom he had made a daring escape. I was duly impressed, and happy to find when we had dinner together that Weatherbe was not nearly as daunting as he looked. My happiness brimmed over when he told me that he had been disappointed by a friend who had promised to accompany him on a traverse through the northern mountains and down the valley of the Lohit Brahmaputra into Assam. He was looking for another companion and asked if I would like to go with him. His journey would take him through the Golden Plain.

It did not take me long to make the necessary arrangements with my Sahmaw employers. Planters' creepers were two a penny, and they were fully aware that my heart really lay in the Kachin country. They were good enough to give me a few months' pay and wish me luck on my journey. The D.C., however, was a tougher nut to crack. My quick decision to accompany Weatherbe merely confirmed his suspicion that I was an irresponsible oddball who needed watching. He first claimed that the Assam Government had reported trouble with the Mishmi tribesmen in the unadministered Lohit valley, and veteod any suggestion of a crossing from our side of the border. Weatherbe countered by saying he would be quite content to go up to Fort Hertz in Khamti Long and spend some time fishing there in the hope that Assam would change its mind. The D.C. then objected to my accompanying Weatherbe even as far as Fort Hertz on the grounds that I had just had malaria, and if it recurred up-country I might be a nuisance to the frontier officials. It took a threat from Weatherbe that he would go to a higher authority to make him change his mind and withdraw his objections.

The following days were a whirl of excitement. In 1926 Fort Hertz was twenty-one days' march by mule track from Myitkyina. Everything we needed for two months had to be packed into sixty-pound loads for carriage by mule or, if we could cross the border, by porter. It was not difficult to find mules. Each year hundreds came down from the hinterlands of Yunnan bearing exotic loads of walnuts and persimmons, smoked hams and pigs' bristles, and not a little opium. Most of these mule trains stayed throughout the cold weather, carrying rations and other supplies to the frontier outposts. Before the rains broke they would go back laden with silk and cotton thread, salt, needles, buttons, cheap necklaces and an occasional carefully hidden load of jade.

At last we were ready to leave, and up before dawn awaiting our mules. I had been warned to expect some confusion when they arrived, but nothing like the chaos which ensued. The first to appear was the head muleteer, smoking a long-stemmed pipe and perched side-saddle on a heap of felt blankets that dwarfed his spindly mount. Then the mules jangled in, the leaders of each muleteer's quartet gaily festooned with bells, mirrors and red-dyed tufts of goats' hair to scare off any devils they might meet on the way. Last of all came the muleteers and their savage furry Chows.

At once pandemonium broke loose. The Chows set upon the *durwan's* guard dogs and my own sheep-dog. The mules, startled by the murderous growls, the yells and flailing sticks and tumbling dogs, fled in all directions. Their blue-clad owners fanned out in hot pursuit, blaspheming furiously, and in an instant the compound was empty again. Luckily for us this was not new to the mules. They knew exactly how far they could run before a crescendo of maniacal screams from the muleteers spelt imminent chastisement. Of a sudden they stopped, and pretended to be grazing industriously, and allowed themselves to be caught and led back as if nothing had happened. No sooner were they tied up and the wooden saddle-frames laid out ready for their loads than fresh confusion arose. The muleteers, seeking light loads, dashed about lifting bedrolls, cases, sacks, and coops of chickens, mixing everything up and hopelessly entangling the rawhide thongs each had carefully laid out. Passionate quarrels broke out while the mules themselves, wisely urinating in preparation for the day's labours, produced fresh howls of anguish from those whose chattels were threatened by the flood. Over an hour passed before we were ready to move. The jingling, tinkling caravan of mules raised a cloud of dust behind us as we marched happily away towards the hills. I felt like Marco Polo.

On the second day we were swallowed by the forest, to travel the rest of the way in the green gully of the mule track, emerging only occasionally on to the banks of a swirling river, or on to a hog's-back from which we caught fleeting glimpses of endless ranges of forested hills stretching as far as the eye could see. But there was plenty to do and see and hear. The rivers teemed with fish, and the turning of every corner promised a shot at a jungle fowl or pheasant for supper. We were hardly ever out of earshot of the whirring flight of the comical hornbills, or that signature tune of the Burma hills, the wild whooping of gibbons.

By day we met small groups of up-river Kachins on the march. The men, though short, were erect and bold-eyed, armed with swords and spears or flintlock guns, their chequered waistcloths worn knee-high to show the strength giving cane rings above their strong calves. None would name his village in case the questioner was seeking vengeance in a blood fued. "Where are you from?" always brought the answer "Over there", with a cock of the chin in the desired direction. They carried light warriors' baskets on their backs, leaving the heavy loads to their womenfolk. The women themselves were lively, and often pretty, and not above exchanging a saucy jest with us as they passed. They made an attractive picture in their calf-length, blue-and-red-striped skirts, tartan breastcloths and head-scarves and huge amber earplugs the size and shape of candles.

Each night we slept at one of the little Public Works rest-houses spaced every twelve miles or so along the track. The Visitors' Books told the story of the frontier life. There were records of shoots and diagrams of every good pool in the nearby rivers, with details of tackle and catches of fish. The names in the books were those of the civil officers and military policemen who lived in the frontier outposts, and the civil engineers and sub-assistant surgeons who looked after their access and their health. No education, or agricultural, or forest or veterinary officer had ever passed that way, nor any civil officer above the rank of district commissioner. It seemed clear that nothing much was done for the hill people beyond keeping the peace. I began to feel sympathy for them and the hardy characters who ruled their remote fastnesses.

We reached Fort Hertz in sixteen days, doing double stages when the mules could stand it. The plain of Khamti Long, in which the little outpost stood, lived up to all my expectations. It lay cupped in tiers of mountain ranges rising to snow-capped peaks on the Tibetan border. Quiet-flowing streams meandered among the towering plumes of bamboo clumps and broad stretches of paddy land. The air was sharp and clean, and a breeze from the northern highlands made us glad of our pullovers, despite the fact that we were well into the hot weather. Above us a myriad white egrets preparing for their annual migration circled and circled in the thermals to gain height until they were no more than a dusting of white dots on the hard blue of the sky, and drifted slowly away towards the Tibetan ranges. I took heart from their passage. They would return and perhaps I, too, would come back to this lovely countryside again.

The civil officer in charge of Fort Hertz was H. E. Fisher of the Burma Frontier Service, a quiet man of fifty or so, content with his lot as 'father' of the plains Shans and the Lisu, Nung and Kachin tribes of his domain, which marched with India, Tibet and Yunnan. His military police half-section was away on leave, and the little Indian doctor and the Burmese office clerk completed his English-speaking world. Yet despite his solitude his life was full of interest, and he left such a deep impression on me that I made up my mind to try to get into the Frontier Service and spend my life among the hillmen I had already grown to admire.

Fisher's attitude to the fears of the district commissioner about the Mishmis was typical. "He's talking through his hat," he said. "The Mishmis'll never touch you if you treat them fairly. You'll need about eighteen porters to get over into their country and they'll all be armed as usual. What with your own Kachins and yourselves you'd be a pretty tough bunch to handle if they did want to cut up rough." We worried about what might be said to him if he let us depart, but he just laughed and said that by the time his report got to the D.C. we would be safely in Assam and the heat would be off.

It was not easy to decide which route to take over the border. Weatherbe wanted one that "no white foot had trod", and this ruled out the easiest though highest route over the 14,000-foot Diphuk La, because Kingdon-Ward had passed that way. It also ruled out the lowest pass (the Chaukkan, pass of ill repute in 1942) because Errol Gray had come into Burma that way many years before. This left only two passes, The Hpunggan to the west and the Kronjawng to the north-west. Little was known about either, other than that all the country between Fort Hertz and the passes, and for an unknown distance beyond, was totally uninhabited. Weatherbe chose the Kronjawng route, as it would give us a chance to visit Rima in Tibet if all went well.

We had to move quickly to beat the rains, as the only practicable way up to the pass lay through the valleys of the Nam Yin and the Nam Khamyang. The map showed the latter to be a mere cleft, getting narrower and more uncharted with each day's journey. We guessed it might take us fifteen days to reach inhabited country, and engaged porters accordingly, finding four Kachins, opium smokers to a man, four wild Nungs from the distant valley of the Nam Tamai, and a hunting group of sullen-looking Lisus from the China border. An old toothless Mishmi, who had fled from his enemies into Khamti Long forty years before, volunteered to act as guide and interpreter, because our path would take him past the old home where he wanted to die. A bachelor Gurkha milkman, moved by God knows what strange motive, offered himself as odd-job man. My own redoubtable Kachins completed the party, and soon made it clear to the porters who was going to rule the roost.

Fisher and Pardhy, his tiny Indian surgeon, saw us off with sad faces. Few people visited Fort Hertz, and if the hospitality they showered on us was anything to go by, their need of our company had been great indeed. We strode off in high spirits towards the beckoning ice peaks, down the slope from the little plateau on which the fort stood and through the Shan villages below. The strange Khamti houses looked deserted, like empty roofs on stilts, because all the accommodation is tucked under the sweeping thatch; but the inhabitants were out in force to watch the mad white men wandering off into the unknown. The children dashed in packs round the backs of houses and gardens to catch a second glimpse, and a third, scattering pigs and dogs and chickens in cacophonous confusion. We threw them sweets and hurried on past the last habitations and on and on by dwindling tracks to the last point of the plain, where the mighty Irrawaddy bursts out of the mountains on its thousand-mile journey to the sea.

We climbed to a knoll where we could look back. Save for the narrow gap of plain in the foreground, there was no sign of the hand of man on the encircling hills. Yet a bare half-century earlier, according to Errol Gray, the whole area had been covered with busy fields, the rivers had held a thousand boats. Where seven *sawbwas* had reigned, only the jungle cock crowed. In the intervening years something had gone wrong: the people had lost confidence and were flowing away to the south. I had the youthful confidence to think that if I had had a hand in the administration things would not have been so bad. The lure of service to the hill peoples seemed more attractive than ever.

By afternoon the tracks petered out and we found ourselves floundering amongst monstrous river boulders, some as big as elephants, and our first camp found us little more than five miles from the junction of the Nam Yin with the main river. Some of our porters were lame, all were exhausted and measled with blood-blister fly-bites, reminders to us that until the jungle closed over the shrinking valley our travel would be pretty uncomfortable. Luckily these pests went to sleep with the dusk, but then the mosquitoes took over, and our eyes streamed in the acrid smoke of the greenwood fires we lit to keep them away. Next morning we found that seven of the Lisu porters had vanished in the night, taking our rations with them, and we had to halt while our village policemen went back to Fort Hertz to recruit more.

When they arrived we were disturbed to find that the newcomers were another bunch of trans-border Lisus from China, and a thoroughly truculent and untrustworthy lot they looked. One young buck in particular seemed determined to try our nerves. Every time we called him he would spring to his feet and unsheath his sword with a flashing sweep so that he faced us at the ready, looking as threatening as possible. It was pretty to watch, but an encouragement to the others, so one day when he did it I loosed a round from my .423 Mauser rifle over his head, and thereafter he troubled us no more. We knew we could trust the Kachins and Nungs, but not the Lisus, so we made sure of the waverers by collecting their swords and spears and crossbows each night and stacking them between us in our lean-to-shelter.

Each day as we progressed the glen narrowed and deepened until we saw the sun for only a couple of hours at midday. It was an eerie place; empty of birds and beasts and, after a waterfall, of fish too. One of our worst problems was finding a piece of flat ground big enough to put down a sleeping-bag. Though we got up at four each morning and marched at daylight, it was often late afternoon before we found a place to camp, and the remaining daylight hours were spent making a barricade of ashes or sand to keep away the hordes of leeches which infested the dank jungle around.

Despite the hard going and heavy loads, our Kachin and Nung porters were full of liveliness and fun. Round the camp fires at night they would sing songs and play their jews' harps with consummate skill, imitating the words of their love songs and the sighs and hesitations of their love-making. One had a hilarious party piece in which he pretended to be a respectable elder trying to creep down the bamboo-floored walkway of a long-house from the visitors' fireplace to the maidens' chamber without waking the household. Magawng Gam taught us how to write leaf-letters, stacking leaves in a package in the order in which they were to be read, the last syllable of the name of each leaf giving the words of the letter.

The stream we followed became narrower, deeper, faster and colder as the days passed. High cliff sides were frequent and we had to cross and recross the stream almost continuously, sometimes up to the small porters' chests in water. We could not take to the hillsides, as they ran precipitously up for hundreds of feet and were covered in dense undergrowth. We had one nasty scare when a thunderstorm on the mountains brought down a ten-foot freshet, but we heard the roar in time and managed to scramble up the bank to safety. Two of our porters developed fever from their constant duckings and we had to abandon most of our clothes and a precious bag of rice which we hung on a tree in case any of our porters returning this way should need it.

At last we reached the foot of the spur we guessed might take us up to the pass, and we cut our way fiercely up through the evergreens until we reached an open pine glade where we could rest in the sun. We had not realised before how much the narrow glen had oppressed our spirits. We felt like men released from a dark dungeon, and the porters laughed and sang and danced until they fell exhausted. We camped for the night with the smell of pine needles in our nostrils, free at last from the leeches.

The next morning called for a start long before dawn because one of our men, foraging for firewood the previous night, had discovered near our path a nest of the big orange-headed chocolate hornets whose stings had killed a military policeman from Fort Hertz some months before. We crept by while the insects slept, up through the pines and the rhododendrons till we were scrambling on bare rock. The ridge petered out in a landslide and we had to scramble our way across loose scree that sloped steeply down to an ominous edge, beyond which we could see forest giants dwarfed to matchstick size. With no head for heights, I must have sweated off half a stone by the time we got across and crawled up to the pass. Weatherbe, as the leader of the expedition, was the first white man to cross.

The sight that met us was beautiful beyond belief. Behind us, to the south, steep slopes fell away to leave a breathtaking view across hundreds of miles of jungle-clad hills shimmering in the heat of a sweltering day. We sweated in our thin cotton shirts, revelling in the sunshine. A few more paces round an outcrop of rock and we were hopping with cold in a mid-winter scene of faery brilliance, two feet of snow softening the contours of the shady hollows below us, great blobs of it weighing down the branches of the pines. Ten paces had taken us from tropical warmth to Arctic cold.

The porters were appalled. Some had never seen snow at all, let alone at close quarters. From where they stared in horror the whole landscape seemed a limitless snowfield stretching away to the Tibetan range in the far distance. They refused to go another yard, swearing that no man could live in such a place and that our tales of a route into India must be all lies. We tried cajoling to no avail. We tried a tempestuous show of temper, but equally fruitless. We wrote imaginary orders, which we pressed into the hands of the village policemen with detailed instructions for their delivery, via Fisher and the Burma Government, to the King Emperor himself, so that he should know of the misfortunes of his illustrious subjects and visit his wrath upon those who failed them. This made a light impression, and some began to waver, and at that moment one of the policemen spotted a beautifully decorated bamboo root pipe which some Mishmi hunter had dropped in the snow about fifty feet below. What seemed to be old melted human tracks led downhill beyond it. Doubts fled at this sign of human passage, and we were soon plunging downhill waist-deep in snow, our feet and legs tingling with cold.

A day's march brought us to a deep, moss-brown river which we guessed would be the Ghalum, a major tributary of the Lohit Brahmaputra. It took us some time to find a pool that was not running like a millrace, and we felled a tall tree hoping to make a bridge across it. Unfortunately the tree was just too short, and disappeared under water some twenty feet from the other bank, leaving us an uncomfortable scramble thigh-deep along the hidden trunk. It was amusing to see how it separated the men from the boys among our porters. The Kachins, used to big rivers, crossed without hesitation, leaning against the current, and came back to help the nervous Lisus and Nungs across, chaffing them for their cowardice. We did not feel too happy ourselves, but managed to hide our fears of a ducking, and soon diverted attention by pointing to a small track among the bushes, beside which we camped, expecting at any time to make acquaintance with the Mishmis, about whom we had heard such unpleasant reports.

We had not long to wait. Soon after we started next day we came upon a little group of six women and children, who dropped their loads of firewood and scuttled like goats downhill as soon as they saw us. It took our old Mishmi half an hour to persuade them to come up and accept a handful of the salt we had saved for just such an occasion. They looked small and undernourished, the older women with gnarled pendulous goitres and the children with abdomens swollen like footballs. From what they said it did not seem as if we should have any trouble with the Mishmis, and we pushed blithely on until we came out upon a great grassy spur bathed in sunshine. To our left the Ghalum flowed down steeply to meet an emerald-green snow river that made a sharp right-angled turn to the west far below us. We could see forty or fifty miles up its deep cleft of a valley, far into the recesses of Tibet. It could only be the Zayul Chu, main stream of the Lohit Brahmaputra. We had reached our first goal.

To the west of us a large Mishmi village sheltered under a steep crag, and as we were on half-rations we decided to spend the night there and see if we could buy replenishments. A furious and somewhat alarming hubbub greeted our arrival. Men rushed up from all directions, more heavily armed, it seemed to us, than any people we had ever seen. Each wore two swords, a long sword on the left side and a dirk on the right; and each carried an immensely long spear or a flintlock gun. We were about to adopt an attitude of truculent defiance when the women and children swarmed round after them, and we realised that this formidable armoury was part of their normal dress. Our old Mishmi explained our presence, and was immediately surrounded by a gaggle of eager questioners trying to find out who he was and where he had come from. We were led away to a house on the outskirts of the village and given the freedom of the veranda to camp, and a rough but welcome meal of millet and bear's meat.

After a decent interval the chief and his elders arrived to tell us with regret that they could not spare any food to us. We had arrived at the end of the hunger season, when all the surplus grain had been used up in the cold-weather feasts, and little remained but the seed grain for the next planting. We brought out a bag of silver and rattled it in front of them, hoping to excite their cupidity, but they just laughed and called out to a group of girls in the background to show themselves. We took the point. They were festooned in silver — silver bangles, silver necklaces and waistbands and broad silver headbands. It appeared that when the Assam Expedition to Rima some years before passed their way they had been required to dig a mule track and had been paid in silver rupees. Since the nearest shop was many days' march away, all the silver had ended up as ornaments for the ladies. Our money was useless.

We had just given up trying to bargain when our Gurkha handyman happened to chuck out one of the small jars that had held our bacon. The dignified elders threw their blankets aside and joined in a mad scramble for the rolling jar, and we realised we were back in business. Where two rupees could not have bought a chicken, an empty jar bought two. We ransacked the baskets of our porters to reclaim all the jars and tins they had begged off us on the way, and bought ourselves enough millet and beans and chickens to last a few days, sealing the bargains with a large jar of maize beer provided by the chief, who got very drunk because by custom he was given the first and most potent draughts.

Before leaving the next day we handed round generous gifts, for we knew that Kingdon-Ward intended to come this way after his plant hunting expedition on the Tibeto-Chinese borderland. Weatherbe took an impish delight in giving the chief his visiting card and asking him to be sure to hand it to the white man who would be coming down from Rima. He knew Kingdon-Ward would be upset to find that he was not the first to complete the traverse by land from China to India. He was upset, and expressed his feelings in some acid comments about Weatherbe in *The Geographical Journal* later that year. We left among shouts of goodwill to make the steep descent to the Zayul Chu, where we were told we could follow the remains of the old mule track down to Sadiya in Assam. I have often thought of that village with sadness. In 1942 an enormous earthquake shook the Lohit valley. A photograph taken by Kingdon-Ward shortly afterwards showed that entire hillsides had been shaken free of trees, soil and villages. I wonder if our friendly acquaintances survived.

Despite our lightening loads, the steep track down to the river tired us more than we had expected. Weatherbe was still feeling weak after fever and had given up all thought of journeying eastwards to Rima. I was beginning to suffer, as were a number of our porters, from jungle sores caused by leech bites. We were all looking forward to the day when we could rest in comfort and nurse our wounds. By mid-morning we reached the river, and collapsed on the trackside, dismayed.

The emerald water swirled tempestuously through a gorge fifty feet below us. There was no path on our side. Across the gorge, perhaps two hundred feet wide, there was stretched a tenuous rope of spliced canes, sagging twenty feet or so in the middle. It was the bridge we had to cross. This crisis, like the first crossing of the Ghalum, again separated the men from the boys among us, but in quite a different way. This time it was the Kachins and ourselves who blanched, while the Nungs and the Lisus prepared happily to shin over. They had monkey bridges in their country, too, and knew what to do about them. They pointed to a bunch of cane rings held by a hook at our end of the bridge and said "Get into one and walk across."

We were still hesitating when a couple of men appeared on the other bank. They swung themselves upside down into a ring apiece, swooped with cocked-up legs to the bottom of the sag, and literally walked up the rope like monkeys till they stood beside us. One of them, a carbine slung on his back, saluted and reported that he had been sent by T. P. O'Callaghan, the Political Officer in Sadiya, to welcome us to his "lands beyond the river" and give what help he could. He carried letters for us, some packets of cigarettes, and a bottle of Scotch. O'Callaghan was obviously a man of the right calibre.

The days down the derelict mule track were dismal in the extreme. The 'little rains' had begun, and we were soaked from morning till night. We slithered and slipped where the Mishmi short cuts dived down into the innumerable gullies which the mule track circled in great loops. Three of our men were tottering with malaria, one had dysentery, and I had developed blood-poisoning in my left leg, which was beginning to swell unpleasantly. Our thoughts marked time till the glorious morning when we turned a corner and saw the 'end of the track' in Assam, the little white bungalow at Theronliang, thrice-blessed harbinger of hot baths and dry beds. Further messages and supplies awaited us there, including a couple of bottles of beer which disappeared in one gulp apiece in salute to their donor, a Captain Kirwan of the Assam Rifles.

In arranging for the return of our porters by a more comfortable route, we had time to consider their qualities. The Lisus had been tough and capable and had done much to help our rations with their crossbows. But they had been aloof and surly, not a little given to, and attracting, suspicion. The Kachins and Nungs, on the other hand, had been open and cheerful, happy in our company, trusting and trustworthy. When we remarked on these differences the Kachins explained them away by saying that it was simply a matter of which side of the China border one came from. In British territory taxes were light, justice lenient and administration straightforward. On the Chinese side rapacious landlords and many levels of officials, to say nothing of wandering bandit gangs, all took their toll of the wretched villagers. Justice depended on how much one could pay, few could trust their neighbours. It was only natural, they said, that the Lisus should be suspicious of everyone. I thought again of the lovely Burma hills and the gay scallywags who lived there, and wondered again if I would ever be able to live among them.

Back in Rangoon a few weeks later, recovered from my blood-poisoning, I was knocking at the door of the Chief Secretary to the Government of Burma, asking to be allowed to join the Burma Frontier Service. There were difficulties. It was argued that my educational qualifications were inadequate, that only graduates were being accepted at the time. I countered placatingly that I was really quite a good bargain despite my lack of a degree. I knew Burma from south to far north. I spoke Burmese, Hindustani and Kachin. I had worked with both plains and hill peoples and got on well with them, and to that extent authority would not be buying a pig in a poke as it would with a young man fresh from home. For good measure I added that I had tested myself against the worst that the jungle could offer and still wanted to live in the hills. There was no risk that I, like some others in the past, would commit suicide through loneliness or boredom. Lastly, but not least important in that Treasury-haunted *ménage,* I asked them to note that I was on the spot and they could save a fare from England. After much huffing and puffing, they opened the back door and let me in, and I spent twenty happy years looking after my beloved highlanders.

H. N. C. STEVENSON, O.B.E., B.Litt.

Noel Stevenson says that the Government of Burma "opened the back door" to let him in to their Frontier Service. That was in 1926. Twenty years later he was very much at the front door as head of the Frontier Areas Administration, having served in Kachin, Naga, Chin and Shan country. He is the author of several works on the hill peoples of Burma's frontiers.

Noel went to Burma in 1923 at the age of nineteen and after working for two years on a rubber estate in the Mergui Archipelago he went to a sugar plantation at Sahmaw, 1,000 miles to the north, where he first came in contact with the Kachins and became deeply attached to them. His appointment to the Burma Frontier Service followed.

When the Japanese invaded Burma in 1941 Noel was ordered by the Governor, Sir Reginald Dorman-Smith, to raise levies throughout the hill areas. He was commissioned in the rank of Lieut. Colonel and began a process which ultimately developed into large forces of Karen, Kachin and Chin levies operating in their own territories. For his notable service he was awarded the O.B.E.

At the end of hostilities in 1945 he became Governor's Secretary to Dorman-Smith and was appointed Director of the Frontier Areas the following year. But having fought for a better future for the hill peoples in these last turbulent years of British rule he resigned in 1947, refusing to be party to plans for the frontier areas which he believed would lead to civil war. Subsequent events have shown that his fears were well founded.

Back in Britain, he took a degree in Social Anthropology at Oxford and lectured for seven years at Glasgow University. He also became well known as a BBC broadcaster. In 1957 he joined Independent Television and was appointed Managing Director of Scottish Television in 1961.

Noel retired in 1965 and since then he and his wife Miggie have been living in the Wigtownshire homeland of his forbears.

FOUR

RICE, PADDY — AND SOME BYE-PRODUCTS

by Christopher Lorimer

I remember W. T. Howison, General Manager in Burma and later a Director of the great merchant house of Steel Brothers and Company, saying of the rice and paddy markets that you have had to be right three times out of five to stay in business. The rice trade was tough going and many failed to stay the course.

Before the turn of the century rice milling was a very profitable business; but more and more mills were built, mostly out in Burma's paddy growing areas, which led to over capacity. The "Big Millers" were mainly British, with mills in the sea ports of Rangoon, Bassein, Moulmein and Akyab. "Small Millers" in the *jungle,* the term used for areas other than the ports, were Burmese, Chinese and Indian. Mill staffs came from Chittagong, but the "Big Mill" engineers were nearly all Scots, to a great extent due to the fact that the world's finest rice mill machinery was made in Kirkcaldy. The saying "they ran their mill on the smell of an oily rag" was true of the Scottish engineers, for the mills burnt their own production of paddy husk to fire the steam boilers. The steam engines which powered the mills also drove electric dynamos, so fuel costs were nil.

Burma pre-1941 produced the largest surplus of rice in the world, exporting some 3½ million tons annually, of which one million tons was shipped to India. The local population, even augmented as it was by a large number of settlers from the Indian sub-continent, could not cope with the harvesting, milling and shipping of the crop, and every year a massive migration of labour took place. They came in thousands from Madras, whence a deck passage by the British India Company's steamers to Rangoon cost in these days five rupees, the equivalent of 37½p for 1,100 miles. From Chittagong also they came to augment the already large Chittagonian community in the Irrawaddy delta; some stayed and settled but most returned home each year. During the busy months, from January to April, every available paddy gig and cargo boat was manned and mill staffs were doubled as every mill in Burma worked round the clock.

This influx of labour, literally in tens of thousands, and their return to their homelands, was said at the time to be the largest annual migration of people taking place anywhere in the world. British, and to a lesser extent Indian, shipping companies provided deck passages for them all and carried off much of the newly milled rice crop. It was a common sight in the season to see over twenty B. I. Company ships strung out at buoys in Rangoon harbour loading rice. Burma and rice were synonymous, world records commonplace. (Today Burma still produces large quantities of rice, but the population has doubled, from 17 to 35 million, since the pre-war days and the exportable surplus is small).

The market price for paddy changed all the time. It was bought in the jungle by Burmese and Chinese brokers, and transported by bullock carts and boats to the main buying stations, then shipped to the mills. This was done in large 50 ton paddy gigs, by Irrawaddy Flotilla Company barges, and some by barges owned by the "Big Millers". Barges were costly and loading would commence at any time of day or night, the towing barge or tug siren signalling arrival. Everyone concerned turned out, including the Burmese girls who carried the paddy baskets. They flocked in from neighbouring villages.

In the depression which followed the world slump in the late 1920s the trade went through a very difficult period. Up to that time paddy for the big mills had been bought through brokers. Each mill had its own team of four or five brokers, powerful people some of whom owned their own paddy gigs. But the severe competition and adverse trading conditions of the 1930s made it impossible for the brokers to buy paddy in the jungle, load it, transport it to the mills and sell at a price which left them any margin.

At that time I was Manager of Steel Brothers' Lower Kanaungtoe rice mill, one of their five big mills in or near Rangoon. I had four of the best Chinese brokers and a very good Burmese broker called U Mya Tha Htun. He was an old fashioned Burman with long hair tied up in a knot underneath his pink silk *gaung-baung*. Mya Tha Htun was a pious and devout Buddhist, honest and reliable, typical of all that was best in Burma. But in business he gave nothing away. At one time I

Paddy gigs awaiting the tide.

A rice mill in the delta.

was doubtful whether we were getting an outturn[1] from him, so I stored 90,000 of his baskets separately. After three days milling when there was only a tiny pile of paddy left I went to the godown to see it. My Chittagonian paddy sircar, the head man in charge of stocks, had reckoned that it was going to be "a close run thing". I went back to the office and anxiously awaited the sircar. After a few minutes he came in smiling and handed me the usual slip of paper. There was an excess of three baskets!

Able though they were, two of my Chinese brokers failed. They were also excellent men and we were staggered by these failures, which were not the only ones. Another Chinese broker at a Steels mill disappeared to China owing the Company over a *lakh* of rupes, equal to the large sum in these days of £7,500.

There was only one thing for it. We, Steel Brothers, must go out to the jungle ourselves and buy paddy, so it was decided to transfer some of the mill managers to handle this work. The thrilling and exciting challenge was accepted by those of us chosen, which included myself.

The pioneer of jungle paddy buying was J. B. (Nobby) Clark, a mill manager, who went in 1929 to Daunggyi on the Irrawaddy near Henzada and set up there the first centre for our new venture. Nobby had been in Burma for four years by then and already spoke Burmese well. He quickly developed a *modus operandi* and was soon able to pass on his experience to the rest of us as we established a network of buying stations throughout the delta.

Nobby had good looks and an extraordinary magnetism. His ability to join in the Burmese addiction to pun making endeared him to the local people and I have seen rows of Burmans waiting patiently for hours on end to speak to him, returning the next day if they failed to get an "audience". Somehow he did not appear at all eccentric in having at the junior end of his Burmese house staff a boy to look after his dog and another to wind his gramophone.

I learnt my paddy buying at Pyapon, in the heart of the delta, under Nobby, finding that he had rapidly become a great master of the art. He had a natural flair for it, making quick decisions based on a readiness to take a view of the market. He blazed the paddy buying trail for Steels driving a high powered speedboat, the houseflag, red with a white St. Andrew's cross, flying on the

[1]One standard basket of 46 lbs. paddy was expected to yield 34.10 lbs of rice, broken rice and bran. The rest was husk and dust.

Burmese girls piling paddy at a buying station.

The rigours of rice growing. Transplanting paddy in a delta field.

bow. More speedboats were ordered and became a familiar sight all over Burma's great rice growing delta as we spread our paddy buying network. We began to feel part of the real Burma, like our Steels colleagues in the teak forests; they had elephants for transport, we had speedboats.

We finally had sixty buying stations and bought close on 31 million baskets of paddy a year, equivalent to some 470,000 tons of milled rice. The stations consisted of about one acre of paddy land next to the river, flattened out after the rains to form measuring and storage space. There was also parking space for about fifty bullock carts, preferably in a shady spot. The station would have a jetty and a small bamboo office with a cool palm leaf roof, where accounts were settled and advances paid out against fresh contracts.

To prevent collusion when paddy was being delivered or shipped we employed a Burmese Buddhist clerk and two Indians, one a Mohammedan at the weighing scale, the other a Hindu counting the tally sticks. Stick were a secure and simple way of counting acceptable to buyer and seller and, most important, to the Burmese girls who carried the baskets of paddy on their heads and were paid at so much per 100 baskets. The cultivator received a fair price for his paddy; there was enough competition from jungle small millers to ensure that. But of course it was impossible to foretell which way the market was going. Some Burmans believed that I knew and when they asked me if it was going up or going down my stock answer was *"Paya bè thi dai"* (only the Lord Buddha knows).

One was constantly reminded of the man who was sent to watch the cotton market by a group of cotton mills in U.S.A. After he had been away for about a fortnight he sent the following telegram to his principals:—

"Some think it will go up. Some think it will go down. I do too. Act at once whatever you do will be wrong."

Pyapon had become an important paddy centre in the delta even before Steels began their paddy buying activities. Lawrence Dawson, a barrister-at-law who had practised in Rangoon, founded a land bank there after the First World War. Dawson's Bank had the laudable object of making advances to Burmese farmers at more reasonable interest rates than those charged by the usurious Indian Chettyars. The collateral of the farmers was their paddy fields. All went well until the slump, when paddy prices fell disastrously and the borrowers found themselves unable to repay the advances, due every year after the harvest.

Dawson's Bank were forced to foreclose and became the reluctant owners of large tracts of paddy lands running into thousands of acres. They had to build a huge godown for the paddy which they collected as rent and usually sold to Steels. I can remember Dawson saying to me, "Nobby always seems to give me a very good price at the time he buys, but then a few days later the market goes up and the price doesn't look so good."

Lawrence Dawson had three other British managers in his bank at Pyapon when I was there. Ted Heaton was the General Manager, a Liverpudlian and a shrewd customer who had the immense satisfaction of outwitting the Japanese in 1942. There was a large amount of gold jewellery in the possession of the delta farmers and this became the collateral for Dawson's advances after the collapse of paddy prices. It would be redeemed after the harvest in time for festivals, etc., but Dawson's had much of it in February 1942, when they had to flee north. Ted took the gold and meeting some friends in Upper Burma who were about to bury their valuables near a jungle village asked if he could put "a few things" which would not be damaged by dampness under the concrete foundation they were making in their cache. When they returned after the war to retrieve their valuables, all were gone except the gold of Dawson's Bank which still lay undisturbed under the concrete.

Burmese place names, particularly in the lower delta, always fascinated me, none more so than Meinma-hla-gyun (beautiful girl island). It was down by the sea, and passing by speedboat one day I asked my Burmese head clerk how the island came by its name. The story is worth re-telling.

"Many years ago a young man in Upper Burma who could find no work there decided to seek his fortune in the fertile lands of the south. He set off in his own canoe from his village near Mandalay. He paddled steadily on and on, day after day, resting every night at a monastery. He had covered close on 600 miles when at Pantanaw, where the worst paddy in Burma grows, some monks advised him to turn westwards to where the superior Meedoung paddy thrives. This is a round grain, a very heavy cropper.

"Eventually he found himself in the Bogale River, not far

from the sea, where he was astonished to find that the river was running the wrong way. He had never heard of tides. Greatly puzzled he made for the nearest land, which happened to be the enchanting little island Meinma-hla-gyun (but it had no name for him then). Tying up his canoe and cautiously venturing inland he heard footsteps and suddenly there emerged from a bamboo forest the most beautiful girl he had ever seen, wearing a white gardenia in her jet black hair. He instandly fell in love with her and when she heard of his long journey how could she resist one so enterprising and bold as to have paddled his canoe all the way from Mandalay.

"He carried the bundle of firewood which the girl had been collecting to her home and met her parents who offered the weary traveller hospitality according to Burmese custom. Soon the couple were married and it was the Upper Burman who gave the island its name.

"And of course they lived happily ever after."

A great advantage of paddy buying in Lower Burma was that it took one, in the course of work, to some excellent snipe grounds. Shooting snipe, and other game birds, was not reserved and permission from the landowners was all that was necessary. I never knew of it being withheld. But our British addiction to shooting such small birds perplexed the local Burmese people, firing off as we did so many cartridges in the process. They called snipe *bo tsa hnget,* which means "the bird eaten by the European", or *sa'naik*, near enough to the English to leave some doubt as to whether the snipe had a name at all before we came on the scene.

I found the best snipe grounds in the delta were *kwins,* fields which were common grazing ground for cattle and buffaloes. There was always a lot of water about, making it impractical to work with gun dogs. Three or four guns was the ideal number and we had beaters who walked in line with the guns; their most important function was to mark the birds as they fell. You had to be so alert that you could not mark your dead birds and at the same time be ready for other snipe rising.

I recall a remarkable, but not entirely untypical, weekend snipe shoot at a place in the delta called Kadonkani. Eric Mackay, Steels paddy buying man at Bogale, and I were due to visit Kadonkani together, so we planned to join forces for a weekend with a friend from the Imperial Tobacco Company, Guy Summerscales who was often in the delta (by speedboat, a means of quick travel which they and Irrawaddy Flotilla men on tour had also adopted) and he brought to meet us from Rangoon a friend who proved to be an interesting addition to the party. John (Tiny) Gladstone was 6′7″ tall, a giant of a man in every way who seemed to be about the last person to be out shooting at the diminutive snipe. But he had learned all there was to know about game shooting from his father Sir Hugh Gladstone of Capenoch, a famous ornithologist and authority on the subject.

Weather and ground conditions had to be just right or snipe would not be there. They were not on that Saturday afternoon and after a long beat Eric gave up and went off to shoot pigeon. Guy, Tiny and I changed direction and continued. Suddenly, "bang, bang", and with a beautiful "right and left" Tiny had the first couple. In half an hour we had 32 birds. Eric was a sad man when he returned with one pigeon!

As organiser of the shoot I had a problem, where to shoot the second day, for it would be useless to go over the same ground again. Our beaters offered to take us to another ground "quite near" by their way of it. It was a Burmese failing that the description of a distance was related to the particular advantage which would accrue to those making the estimate. This was no exception and no precise answer was forthcoming as to where we were going when we set off with the beaters in our speed-boats. The reason was soon clear as we approached the village of Eywa, tied up our boats and began walking towards the nearby grazing ground. But first I had to appeal to Guy to bring with him as many cigarettes as he had and come into the village with me to placate the villagers. Fortunately he had several hundreds and these were handed out and at least an argument, if not an incident, avoided. The fact was that the Eywa villagers should have been asked to provide beaters, but the wily men of Kadonkani wanted another day of the sport and amusement, not to mention the pay, which a snipe shoot provided.

Eywa, like Kadonkani, was close to an open estuary and as we started our beat we could hear the waves lapping on the beach. Great belts of rich green jungle and palms surrounded the grazing ground, the sun was shining between beautiful white cloud formations and everything was perfect — except that again there were no snipe. As the day wore on and I began to despair there was suddenly a thrilling moment as we tried an unbeaten area and found damp ground. "Wisps" of snipe began to rise and three of us had immediate "rights and lefts". The most perfect hour of shooting that I had ever experienced in Burma followed, and a fair bag of 49 birds. Later the Eywa headman told me that the ground had not been shot over for ten years; I wonder if it has been shot over since.

When we reassembled at the Kadonkani dak bungalow that evening and totted up our expenses for the shoot, which included food, drink, bungalow charge and beaters, each share came to the equivalent of £2. It was 1934.

I was posted in 1939 to Henzada on the main Irrawaddy in charge of Steels paddy buying operations there. My new territory stretched for 109 miles from the village of Thetpangone, south of Henzada, to Thaledan, a few miles below Prome. It was a complete change from the lower delta; touring on the broad waters of the Irrawaddy in the cold weather of January and February was a sheer joy. But the responsibilities were still there, ever present.

I had a .45 Colt revolver which lay on top of our cash in a small leather despatch case containing anything up to the equivalent of £10,000 in ten rupee notes. The theory was that in a "your money or your life" situation I would open the despatch case as if to hand over the cash but shoot the robber instead. But law and order were so good in Burma in those days that I was fortunately never put to the test.

There was variety in my paddy buying journeys from Henzada. Most frequently I went to the riverine stations by speedboat, but to reach some areas I travelled by motor car or by train and even by pony trap to one out of the way place.

I had to go on what was described as a slow mixed train from Henzada to a station called Kyangin. Slow it was, averaging 14½ miles an hour for the 65 mile journey, but it suited me well, for stops at stations were long enough to enable me to transact business.

The only way I could reach one paddy buying station was by pony trap on an earth track. This was a delight, a silent journey with the beat of the pony's hoofs almost inaudible. The country Burmese looked after their animals and we always stopped to rest our pony under a thick grove of trees. On arrival the buying process could not be hurried, the landowners wanting to gossip on every subject but paddy before business could be done. I had become a collector of old Burmese weights and it was here that I acquired the tiniest, which my landowner friend told me were for weighing jewellery. Burmese Kings, with the advice of astrologers, issued standard weights in the forms of birds and animals, including the mythical lion the Chinthé. So all that could be found, and acquired, were collectors items.

Steels Forest Manager at Thayetmyo was Bill Cruikshank whom I sometimes met at Prome when I went there to perform one particular journey. One night we became so involved at the Prome Club playing snooker and enjoying a few drinks that we didn't get back to the Chummery until 4 a.m. When I dropped off to sleep Bill was still talking to me and I had no more than ten minutes in bed as I had left instructions to be wakened at 4.30 a.m. I set off with my head clerk at once in an old open touring car going about ten miles down a good tarred road out of Prome, then took to a rough and dusty bullock cart track at slow speed. By dawn we reached a small creek where two canoes were waiting, one for me and one for the clerk. We were paddled down this narrow creek for four miles to the village of Kyithe which is on he left bank of the Irrawaddy south of Prome. This was our destination and business over we caught an Irrawaddy Flotilla steamer which called at 8 a.m. and was why such an early start had to be made. Returning by canoe and road was out, as the canoes would have been a long time in the creek against its strong current.

About once every ten days I went to Htonbo, some thirty miles below Prome on the right bank of the Irrawaddy. It was a long haul by speedboat and I stayed the night at the Government dak bungalow, which was beautifully situated on the edge of the river. On one occasion it was occupied by a Government officer and his family who had come for a holiday. This was not surprising as it was a delightful spot and I had fallen in love with it myself. I decided there and then to build a garden house for myself there at Htonbo and found an idyllic site by the river just south of the village.

Next visit I gave my local broker San Myint a plan and in a few weeks he erected with local labour a two bedroom house. The floor was 3 feet above ground level, bamboo matting walls, bamboo shutters instead of windows and a dunnee palm roof. San Myint even remembered to have the doors made 7 feet high, as I am 6'3". The total cost was 1,000 rupees, £75. And it was shaded during the heat of the day by a group of palm trees and from evil spirits at night by the blessing of a dear old Buddhist priest who came to watch it every day while it was being built.

A garden house is not complete without a garden, so San

Myint planted two rows of orange trees and I supplied seeds of phlox, dianthus, sweet peas, zinnia and sunflower. Sadly the Japanese invasion prevented me from making use of the house for more than a few months. But there was a sequel.

After we were driven out of Burma in 1942 by the Japanese it was a fact to be faced that as part of the British Empire there was no network of intelligence agents left behind in Burma. I had been commissioned into the army in India and found myself in a new Burma section of Intelligence.

Two operations had already gone wrong. In the first an Anglo-Burman ex-policeman, disguised as a Burman, had been dropped into Upper Burma by parachute. The unfortunate man was caught and the Japanese cut his head off. In the second, two Burmans were parachuted in with a wireless transmitter and receiver. They too were captured and were made to transmit messages under duress. But by a pre-arranged code we knew what was happening and bluffed the enemy by sending back what appeared to be genuine messages.

It was against this discouraging background that I was asked to plan a new operation. I reckoned that anywhere in the north of Burma was hopeless as a dropping zone; we were now into late 1943 and Wingate's Chindit operations had made the area like a hornet's nest with the likelihood that anyone we parachuted in would be shot by our own men. So I looked much further south and what better than the area near Htonbo that I knew so well.

For the drop I chose a point on the west bank of the Irrawaddy south of Prome where a loop is made by the road crossing and re-crossing the Henzada / Kyangin railway line. I thought these landmarks would be easy to spot from the air, as indeed they proved to be. I knew that there were flat paddy fields there which would make a good dropping zone. I was pretty sure that the railway would not be working and there was no main road near. Everything should be pretty quiet and free from Japanese. Bad planning would cost the life of a brave man and yield no dividends of intelligence which were so desperately needed.

There was a rule that the officer who knew the dropping area must accompany the agent in the aircraft to make sure that the R.A.F. dropped him in precisely the right place. This did a lot to inspire confidence in our men and the agent chosen for this operation was no exception. Although he was a Burman he knew nothing of that part of his native land. He had been well trained by an officer who had served many years in Burma and was now highly specialised in Intelligence; this man's "bible" was Rudyard Kipling's *Kim* and each of his pupils received a copy as their introduction to "the greatest game in the world", which they themselves were destined to play.

We took off in a Hudson at 1830 just as darkness was falling. It was two days before full moon and the weather was perfect. We were about to cover roughly 1,050 miles and our course would take us less than 100 miles from Mingaladon, the main aerodrome near Rangoon.

As we approached our destination and descended to 300 feet the moon shone so brightly I could see the stubbles of the paddy plants. There was the landmark, the loop made by the road crossing and re-crossing the railway. Our man jumped. He was destined to do a magnificent job and to be picked up two months later by the Navy on the west coast of Burma.

After the drop I asked the Hudson pilot to fly over Htonbo on our way back. Just as he announced, "We are now flying over Captain Lorimer's garden house", we were fired at from the ground and hastily swung west to the safety of the Bay of Bengal.

The last word on Htonbo is that during the 1942 retreat, when Steels evacuated some of their Indian staff via the Taungup Pass to India, the house was used as a staging H.Q. I was never to see it again. For health reasons I had to make up my mind that I never could return to Burma.

CHRISTOPHER LORIMER

I first met Christopher Lorimer in 1934 at Pyapon in the Irrawaddy delta. It was then a small but important township where he lived and worked, paddy buying for Steel Brothers and Company; and he cut a fair dash with his youthful good looks and the smart speedboat in which he travelled over his territory. He was a happy man, loving the delta life, the excitement of the paddy market and above all the Burmese people. He was a complete Burma-phile; he still is.

Born in Edinburgh in 1904, he is the eldest son of a famous father, Sir Robert Lorimer, the great Scottish architect who designed the Thistle Chapel and the National War Memorial in the capital city. Christopher was reading architecture at Cambridge University when the opportunity came to join Steel Brothers. It was 1925 and prospects then for architects were so poor that he decided there would be a better future in business; and Steels offered a wide variety of career with interests in Burma in rice, timber, oil and other trading activities.

He spent his first years as a rice mill manager in Rangoon but his love of the country developed in the real Burma of the delta paddy fields. He and his friend Nobby Clark rented a 28-acre paddy field near Pyapon to further their knowledge of cultivation and its costs, and on a Sunday morning they could be seen wading knee deep through flooded paddy fields studying the ploughing and transplanting. At harvest time they were out with the sickle joining the reaping.

After the war Christopher married and settled in his father's old home Gibliston in Fife. His wife Daria and their three sons and daughter have become accustomed, when he has a visit from a Burma friend, to him switching off from today and living again in those far off days of fifty years ago.

FIVE

FISHY STORY

by Ritchie Gardiner

About 200 miles North of Rangoon — on the proverbial road to Mandalay — lies the town of Toungoo. To the East of this, across the Sittang River, the land rises into a series of jungle clad hills. They are peopled by Karens whose small villages generally lie near the hill tops. Through this area runs another river which was known to contain mahseer, anything from two to about ten lbs. in weight. It was very seldom visited by Europeans, for there were no roads and you needed elephants to transport your camping equipment.

To those who are not acquainted with the mahseer it may come as a surprise when I say that weight for weight it is generally considered to be stronger and rougher than a salmon. Although it belongs to the carp family (barbus tor) and is normally a bottom feeder, it was generally fished for by spinning with an extra strong spoon and treble hooks. It has very powerful rubbery lips which can crush an ordinary spoon and its teeth — which incidentally are not unlike a set of human dentures — lie well back in its throat.

Towards the end of the hot weather in April it was the villagers' custom to poison some of the pools in the river. This was done by a squad who stationed themselves at the top end and hammered slabs of bark from a certain tree on the low rocks which projected. The rather frothy juice from this bark had a stunning effect on the fish and when they floated near the top of the water, another squad of men and boys scooped them in. You can imagine the noise and excitement, especially among the boys, each striving to bring in the biggest fish. They were then salted and dried for use in the ensuing year.

I cannot say I envied them in the culinary aspect, for the flesh was rather tasteless and a mahseer always seemed to be a mass of small bones quite unrelated to each other. They could defeat even my very conscientious and painstaking native cook. This method of fishing was well enough known in Burma but was generally frowned on. In the hills, however, it had been the custom from time immemorial and was not interfered with by the Authorities. Indeed, it was an important adjunct to the villagers' diet in a living which at the best could only be described as frugal.

If you wanted to fish for sport the best time was to set out before the "annual poison festival" when the weather was at its hottest and when most Europeans were making for the cooler climate of the hill stations. Some years before the last War, I decided on an expedition to this river which I had only visited once before. I chose a new area and on my first day after settling in camp, I set out to fish. In doing this I broke one of the cardinal forest rules and went alone. In this particular case it so happened that it did not matter, but even in those days I never could abide — and still can't — a man sitting idle on the bank behind me. It was a foolish practice, however, which got me into trouble on at least one other occasion.

I had on heavy ammunition boots and carried a bag of tackle and a long gaff. The gaff, I may say, was another eccentricity of mine, for all the old hands used to say that you could not gaff a mahseer. The reason for this is the fact that it is covered with large thick leathery scales and if a gaff does penetrate, the scale merely comes off on the point. I knew this from hearsay and hitherto I had always used a net, but I thought that if I had an extra sharp gaff and used it on the belly instead of the back, it would fully penetrate a fish. I was armed this day with a gaff sharpened by our blacksmith to a needle point.

Not long after starting I came to a pool about 300 yards long, deep and rocky. I waded in at the head to knee deep. Not far below me on my side the bank rose to a cliff, but on the other side across about 20 yards of deep and strongly running water there was a fair beach extending down the pool. At my third cast a fish struck. When I say "struck", I mean it, for a mahseer hits so hard that it can pull the rod out of your hands, if you are off your guard. I braked hard on the Silex reel but it hadn't the slightest effect and after a few seconds I saw to my consternation that I had an almost bare drum. The fish had taken just under 100 yards of line in one quite unstoppable run.

There were two alternatives, to hold and break, or to follow and hope.

Being then young and foolish I immediately chose the latter, whipped the cork handle of the rod into my mouth and plunged downstream making diagonally for the opposite bank. I can swim but I would never describe myself as a strong swimmer and to set off as I did, encumbered with heavy boots, a bag and a gaff plus a rod in my mouth and a sun helmet on my head was, to say the least of it, taking a risk. Half way across I became well aware of this as I was beginning to ship water. I really thought I had had it and was rapidly weakening when I kicked for the bottom and just got a touch with one foot. This gave me the necessary fillip to struggle the few more strokes to come waist deep and wade ashore, where I collapsed on the gravel. But I still hung on to the rod, though I was too exhausted to know or care what was happening at the other end.

After some minutes trembling and coughing up water I recovered enough to stand up and try the line. It was fast, but fast to some immovable object. I followed downstream reeling in but putting on no pressure until I came opposite the snag, for snagged it was. On tightening however, there was a curious drumming on the line which I felt was not caused by the water, which at this point had a very slow flow and was probably 20 feet deep. Try as I could nothing would shift it so I sat down again — very willingly — wondering whether I should break there and then or try some stones, just in case the fish was still on. I do not remember whether I left the line loose at this point but whilst pondering and resting I suddenly saw to my surprise that it moved. The fish was on and clear of the snag, and I had this time the advantage of a beach where I could follow it.

About ten minutes later after several fierce runs I was able to bring it close enough to see that it was well over the 10 lbs. that I had thought it to be. With some trepidation I unslung the gaff and went firmly for the belly and the — hopefully — soft scales. It happened exactly as the old hands had predicted, though I had struck really hard. The gaff just bounced off with one large scale embedded on it, and the fish shot away taking about 60 or 70 yards of line before I could throw the gaff away and catch up to come level again. It was another battle but not quite so strenuous this time, and having decided the gaff was out I played it to a point where I could beach it, which was successfully managed at last. It would be untrue to say that I was more exhausted than the fish, but it crossed my mind at the end that it would not take much effort on its part to pull me into the water!

It weighed a mere 18 lbs. which, though it was easily a record for that river, would be a tiddler compared to the big fellows which used to be caught up above Myitkyina.

More than once I have been asked what I would do in like circumstances with a salmon. Today, I can safely say that age and cold water would suggest a more prudent course of action.

J. R. GARDINER G.M., O.B.E.

Ritchie Gardiner admits to having been young and foolish when he pursued an 18 lbs. mahseer into a river in the Karen Hills. High up in the Irrawaddy, where the mahseer can come up to 60 lbs., he would have been more cautious.

But he was never one to take the easy road and his later story of marching out of Burma in 1942 through the Chaukkan Pass reveals even more of the man he is. Born and bred in Ayrshire, Ritchie worked underground in a coal mine in his youth while taking a degree at Glasgow University in Mining Engineering. An opportunity to go to the forests of Burma came to him in 1925 and he went out to join MacGregor and Company.

He soon made his mark. In 1937 he was appointed Manager of all the forest operations of MacGregors, with a labour force of between two and three thousand and some 600 elephants. He also represented the European community on the Municipal Corporation of Rangoon.

In his Chaukkan story he makes but brief mention of his rescue of John Fraser from a river in torrent. For this action he was awarded the George Medal. Later in the war, back in India, he was first posted to the Burma Intelligence Corps and shortly after became head of the Burma Section of Force 136, the Far East branch of Special Operations Executive. For his work there he was appointed O.B.E. An official history of Force 136 has recently been authorised and will tell of the gallant men who carried out operations behind the Japanese lines.

After the war Ritchie returned to Ayrshire and took up farming. There he and his wife Mary have brought up their family of three sons and a daughter. There is now a lawyer and another engineer in the family and it is no surprise to me that his youngest son is a Captain in the Royal Marines and enjoys a varied set of activities in which I am sure his father would have revelled in his youth.

SIX

BY THE CHINDWIN AT PEACE

by Alister McCrae

For the retreating army the wide river was the last obstacle to be overcome if they were to escape the relentless pursuit of the Japanese enemy. Months of withdrawal had brought the British force to the Chindwin in May 1942; India was their goal. They were ferried across by steamers of the Irrawaddy Flotilla, hurrying on, for the south-west monsoon rains were imminent. There was no time to do other than curse the delay and the very existence of this river. There was certainly no time to admire the scenery.

Yet the Chindwin is the loveliest of rivers and it is a lifeline for the people of the region through which it flows. Away from the flat delta, where it joins the Irrawaddy below Mandalay, the scenery can be quite dramatic, and approaching the upper reaches a majestic panorama unfolds. To westward the Chin Hills rise behind a narrow plain through which the Myittha River winds its way into the Chindwin at Kalewa; and further north, coming up to Homalin, where ends the 400 miles of navigable river*, the Naga Hills tower to north-west as the valley narrows and the 12,557 feet high peak of Saramati, the highest in Burma, appears in the far distance. Beyond there lie the Patkai Hills, source of the Chindwin and an area which, surely with no hint of pride, boasts the wettest climate in the world.

I knew nothing of this remote part of Burma when I was sent there in 1935 to inspect the Chindwin steamer services of the Irrawaddy Flotilla Company and to investigate a reported default by the Homalin sub-Agent. I was in my third year with the Company and had worked only in lower Burma, mainly in the Irrawaddy delta area and had just spent another "rains" there. Over 100 inches of rain falls in the delta in the wet south-west monsoon period from May until October, accompanied by a humidity unbelievable until experienced. It is good for growing

*To be strictly accurate, a small Government administration steamer navigated a further eighty miles up the Chindwin.

paddy but it made for problems of keeping fit. I was already looking forward to the dry and cooler season and the move to upper Burma was doubly welcome; the further north, the colder the weather during the fine north-east monsoon period.

Almost a hundred years ago, in 1885, another British force had taken to a Burma river on steamers of the Irrawaddy Flotilla. But this force advanced against little opposition up the Irrawaddy, took Mandalay, exiled the last King of Burma to India and annexed Upper Burma. When I followed the same river road from Rangoon to the Chindwin in 1935, the year 1885 seemed a very long way behind, just a part of history. Today, as we approach another fifty years on, the whole time scale seems to have shrunk as we realise that our time in Burma was very short. But in 1935 my thoughts were on the present, and on a future which then still seemed to hold out the prospect of quite a few more years of British involvement.

To travel into the Chindwin by river one had to make for Pakokku, a small but prosperous township on the west bank of the Irrawaddy some 100 miles south of Mandalay and a few miles below where the Chindwin delta debouches into the parent river. I travelled up from Rangoon in the luxury of one of the Company's Mandalay mail paddle steamers, the "leviathans of the river", taking in new scenes as I saw the Irrawaddy above Prome for the first time. It was the end of October and the river was still high, a six day passage to Pakokku. There I disembarked and joined the waiting Chindwin sternwheeler.

The Chindwin was served entirely by sternwheelers, our fleet of thirteen in all. Only they could cope with the low water season channels; with their light steel hulls and even trim (boiler forward and engines aft) they drew unladen less than two feet of water. *Sind,* which was to take me to Homalin, was one of four built by Yarrow and Company in British Columbia during the 1914-18 war, when their Clyde yard was fully engaged on naval construction, and shipped from Canada to Rangoon for re-erection. After some twenty years in service she was in fine condition, but then I had just left a mail steamer (also Clyde built by Denny) which was all of thirty years old and looked good for another thirty. *Sind,* 132 feet in length (the mail steamer was 326 feet) had cabin accommodation for six; she was licensed to carry 800 deck passengers on her two decks, but with much of her upper deck occupied permanently with bazaar stalls she had deck space for less than half that number.

Pre-war. A Chindwin sternwheeler at Kalewa.

Post-war. A modern sternwheeler at a busy ghaut.

Sind was making the last run of that high water season right up to Homalin, a 400 mile passage that took exactly one week. The next sailing, a week later, would go no further than Mawlaik, about two-thirds of the way, and for the following months of low water a smaller sternwheeler would ply on the treacherous upper reaches.

One of my duties, an important one, was to ensure that wood fuel supplies were plentiful; at more than half of the thirty-five stations of call on the Chindwin, firewood contractors kept supplies ready stacked on the river bank. Frequent loading of small quantities of fuel was specially important when the river was low and every inch of displacement was needed for cargo and passengers; supplies were even kept ready at each end of notoriously bad channels, so that fuel could be replenished as soon as the steamer was through. Groundings and the laying out of anchors from the jolly boat to heave the steamer through, an operation that could take a whole day and night, sometimes longer, consumed much fuel.

All the Chindwin sternwheelers fired their boilers with the local wood fuel. Reserves of this timber were set aside by the Forest Department of Government for the contractors to cut their supplies, and these were plentiful in that countryside which seemed to be all jungle from the river to the horizon. The short billets were stacked ready to be measured close to the landing places and villagers, usually women, carried the billets on board on their heads. The Burmese steamer clerk paid on the nail and everyone was happy; and this consumption of large quantities of firewood and the employment generated made something of a virtue out of necessity for the Company.

The smooth operation of the firewood contracts were to be part of my occupation in the months to come. Meantime, I return to that first leisurely journey up the Chindwin which began at Pakokku with the *Sind* well laden to her full draught of four feet. From a map (there were no charts for these changing rivers) I could see that over a stretch of some twenty miles above Pakokku the flat Chindwin delta spreads her waters into several channels as they join the Irrawaddy. I marvelled that our British Captain knew the right one; but for this he took little credit, for the Company's own buoying and pilotage service were responsible for seeing to it that no mistakes were made. This delta created problems when the Chindwin was low and, long before commercial navigation was thought of, the Kings of

Burma were concerned that a navigable route should exist into the Chindwin for their own steamers. One royal person went as far as to have a canal of some length constructed when passage was impeded in the dry season. It was not long before the canal was swept away and disappeared in high water floods.

No problems existed in the month of November and the *Sind* meandered up river through the flat plain to the first night station at Monywa. Monywa is at the end of a railway line from Mandalay; the remainder of the Chindwin to the north was, and no doubt still is, dependent for communication on the river. Here at Monywa the flat plain is already left behind and the Chindwin is flowing through defined banks of a countryside of low hills.

Then, covering 150 miles in three days, the passage up river progressed slowly to Kalewa and the unforgettable mountain scenery of the Chindwin valley unfolded in greater splendour day by day, a continuous peaceful scene disturbed only by the hurly-burly of activity at each stopping place. We were the weekly "mail boat", a travelling bazaar, and the bazaar people on board, permanent passengers, provided the shopping opportunities which none of the riverine villages were large enough to support. They traded too, and could be seen clinching a deal from the ship's rail as we pulled away from a stopping place.

The Captain told me that he had a small party of American tourists for a round trip the previous cold weather. Arriving at Mingin, the second night stop above Monywa, in the late afternoon, the party went ashore to see the fine carvings in an old *hpoongyi-chaung* in the village. They were somewhat taken aback to be shown there a tin coffin full of honey, in which the body of a *Sayadaw* was lying embalmed. It was explained that he was being kept thus until sufficient money was collected for a *hpoongyi-byan,* when the body would be cremated in the traditional Buddhist manner.

The steamer got under way next morning early and at breakfast it was observed that a jar of honey had been added to the usual marmalades, etc. A lady of the American party called the butler. "Where did this honey come from, butler?" she asked. "The honey, Missee," replied the Madrassi butler, obviously proud of his acquisition, "is from the *hpoongyi-chaung* at Mingin." After a stunned silence he was told it would not be required.

Apart from the fine scenery, the river itself did not seem particularly remarkable between Monywa and Kalewa during that November passage. But on another later visit in the month

Pagodas by the river.

of June I was to witness the amazing effect of a river in high flood making its stormy passage through two narrow defiles. From the Patkai Hills the Chindwin receives a massive flow of water with the rains and will rise thirty feet in these gorges in the short space of two days, a more sudden flood than the slower surge of the Irrawaddy, which comes from the melting Himalayan snows. Only the powerful sternwheelers can attempt passage through the awesome whirlpools in the gorges and even they may not dare to enter on a sudden high rise. The anvil shaped rock, from which the *Pay-way* Whirlpool below Kalewa takes its name, has thus been shaped by the action of the water and the current at full strength throws a bow wave right across the river, like a large vessel at speed. I was to experience a delay of several days at Monywa in June waiting on a thirty feet rise to settle before any attempt could be made to pass up through the *Shweziyay* Whirlpools some twenty miles up river.

There was more to Kalewa than met the eye. It occupies a promontory at the mouth of the Myittha, a river which gives life to an area of paddy cultivation. *Lonedwin* dug-outs which ply on the Myittha bring their loads of paddy to be transhipped at Kalewa to bamboo rafts and these are floated down to the rice mills of Monywa. At Kalewa too I first heard the chant of the upper Burma waterfront labourers as they warped a heavy piece of machinery off the ship down the gangways to the river bank. The timing was set for a series of short pulls by the chanting of couplets:

Swe-laik	*Swe-laik*	Pull! Pull!
Ah-hnin	*Swe-laik*	A strong pull!
Kyaik-te	*Chit-te*	Liking! Loving!
Chit-te	*Kyaik-te*	Loving! Liking!
Mo-la	*Le-la*	Rain? or Wind?
Le-la	*Mo-la*	Wind? or Rain?
Lu-la	*Kya-la*	Man? or Tiger?
Kya-la	*Lu-la*	Tiger? or Man?
Swe-laik	*Swe-laik*	Pull! Pull!

Kalewa is the mid-point of the navigable river. In these days it marked the end of comfortable travel for Government officials of the Burma Frontier Service, for here they left the steamer for several days journey by *lonedwin* up the Myittha to Kalemyo, to be followed by long marches from there into the hills. Kalewa had assumed a special importance to the life of the Chindwin in the fifty years since the steamer services had begun and the forests opened up for extraction of their valuable teak; and since administration of the Chin Hills had been established. It was the very heart of the river in those peaceful days of 1935.

Yet a mere six years later I was to see this quiet little township as a scene of human tragedy, with refugees in thousands fleeing from the Japanese invasion, streaming ashore from the steamers, hopefully bound for the safety of India. Many were not to survive beyond the notoriously malarial Kabaw valley through which lay the only route to the frontier of Manipur. Then came the retreating British Army crossing the river to Kalewa with the Japanese at their heels and the rain clouds of the monsoon already threatening.

Mawlaik is some forty miles further up river. It was the headquarters of the Upper Chindwin District and I had heard it described as a parasite on the Government. It had no trade and was selected for the District HQ in a patch of jungle which was cleared and a town planned; there would be no malaria (the whole Chindwin had a bad name for being malarious) and people would flock there to live. But the Burmans did not come and it was just a tidy little capital of the District with all the officials and the offices and houses which accompanied them. Nearby there was a famous *jeel* for duck shooting which may have had some influence on the choice of Mawlaik instead of the more obvious communication centre at Kalewa. But it suited also the Bombay Burmah Trading Corporation; a number of their British staff, some with their wives, lived there conveniently near to their Upper Chindwin teak forests.

Our Company's Mawlaik Agent was a Sikh, Rattan Singh. Of all the sixty Agencies throughout the country this was the only one not occupied by a British Assistant or, as in the great majority of cases, by a full time Burmese Agent usually with long service. But Rattan Singh was a good choice in that far off and infrequently visited place. He had held down the appointment for several years and was a man to be reckoned with, for he also ran a store and sold everything that this affluent community required. He was unlikely to put a foot wrong and risk losing the standing he had as Agent for the Flotilla Company. Homalin came under him as a sub-Agency, but he did not have authority to hire or fire; it was his report of a shortage in the cash at Homalin which was taking me there to investigate. He had gone up to check, found the sub-Agent short by two hundred rupees and no explanation to offer. He wanted the man dismissed. It seemed a not unreasonable request.

There was an increasing remoteness about the last 150 miles of river as *Sind* steamed on towards Homalin. But first, a few hours above Mawlaik, we came to Pantha where there was a small, modern oil refinery, and at a jetty taking its product was one of our two river tankers specially built for this traffic. Suitably named *Chintank,* she ran between Pantha and a depot near Monywa for so long as the river permitted, for she was driven by twin screws and drew close on three feet even in light condition.

The crude oil for the Pantha refinery came from a small Field 27 miles inland at Indaw, a fearsome journey during the monsoon rains for the men who won the oil; elephants were the only means of transport then. The telephone line from Indaw to Pantha was of barbed wire to discourage monkeys from swinging on it. But it all must have been worth while, for the Indo-Burma Petroleum Company which owned all this was an off-shoot of Steel Brothers and Company.

The next day I was being shown a channel where our stern-wheeler, during last year's low water, had been forced aground to avoid running into an elephant. A great male tusker, he had paid no heed to the steamer's whistle and meandered up the narrow channel in his own time.

When we came shortly afterwards to Sittaung, a small village on the west bank, I viewed it with special interest, thinking that only an intrepid explorer, or at least an experienced jungle wallah, would attempt the well known 35 miles march from there inland to Tamu, whence a further three days would take him to a motor road and civilisation in Assam. It had in fact been traversed often in both directions and was accepted as the only route into India from Northern Burma, provided one was prepared to rough it a bit. The events of 1942 changed all that; there was no easier way to get to Tamu and into Assam or Manipur, as many who were forced to take alternative routes were to find.

Before reaching Homalin I was to see villages from where paddy from a fertile hinterland was shipped down river in the traditional Chindwin rafts; I was to see the small Shan State of Thoungdoot, where a *Sawbwa* lived and ruled, a veritable enclave in which the Government held no sway; and on a

A group of Nagas who came down from their hills to the Chindwin to work loading firewood to the steamers.

The dak bungalow at Homalin.

shingle bank at the mouth of the Uyu River, just below Homalin, gold washers at work making a meagre living from gold dust of the Uyu, with only the chance of a small nugget to spur them on.

When we came to Homalin in the twilight of a brilliant evening, with the sun just vanished below the western mountains, I found the sub-Agent, Ko Ba Tun, on duty awaiting the steamer's arrival. He was a man in his thirties, smartly turned out in the modern style with a thick cotton *eingyi* over his white collarless shirt and with a cotton *longyi*; he wore no *gaung-baung* over his Western style haircut. We went straight to his office, which was in his house, to check his cash deposit. I knew that if I could not quickly resolve the problem of the shortage found by Rattan Singh I should have to stay in Homalin for a week; *Sind* would sail down next morning at day-break and the next steamer was a week later.

I was somewhat taken aback when the correct amount of cash was produced. When I asked Ba Tun to explain the earlier shortage only a silence followed. I pressed him for an answer, I cajoled, then I grimly threatened instant dismissal, but to no avail. Yet already he had appeared to me to be a good type of Burman and our Captains on the steamers had spoken well of him. Only Rattan Singh condemned him and that I could not ignore.

I decided to stay in Homalin for the inevitable week and to get to the bottom of this. Ba Tun would have to be replaced if I failed to find a good enough reason to keep him on; but I felt that somehow this would be forthcoming, for the appointment as our sub-Agent was prestigious to the holder and he would lose much face in Homalin if he was sacked.

I called on the Sub-divisional Officer and was fortunate to find him in the station, for his duties took him away frequently on tour. He was a Karen, a charming man named Joshua Poo Nyo, and he gave me a warm and friendly welcome, saw to it that I was duly installed in the dak bungalow and invited me to his home for dinner. So I settled in at the dak bungalow; furniture was at a minimum, but it was kept in reasonable cleanliness and the only real problem was keeping warm, for the nights were already cold. But my *lugale* was used to providing for my comfort and we had come prepared, as always, with camp bed, bedding, mosquito net, cooking utensils, stores and all.

Homalin was little more than a large village and I found a new experience in living there, an experience of placid existence and friendships with young Burmese officers of Government whom I joined to play tennis in the evenings. Poo Nyo belonged to the Burma Frontier Service and went off into his charge, which covered a large and sparsely populated area to the north including the Somra Tract of the Naga Hills. Large areas were entirely unpopulated and abounded with elephant, tiger, leopard and deer, and wildfowl from pelicans to peacocks. His predecessor, not many years before, had to mount a punitive expedition to deal with unadministered Nagas who had raided the territory and departed with some heads, human ones; for there were still head-hunters in the Naga Hills.

Poo Nyo's parents lived with him and with his father I found a special rapport. He would be in his fifties and very active, eager always for a long walk or to take me off to shoot snipe. Although I had met Karens in the delta, it was through knowing the Poo Nyos that I became aware for the first time of a great affection for them; in later years this became admiration also for their loyal service in war time.

As the end of the week approached I was no further on, despite daily questioning, with the unyielding Ko Ba Tun. Yet I was otherwise impressed by what I saw of him and undoubtedly he commanded some respect in the little community. He had not a lot to do for us, being also a part time and trusted clerk for a small rice merchant, his main duty being to deliver the cargoes left by the weekly steamer and collect the freight charges. On my part, I kept hoping that repeated threats of dismissal would produce some explanation of his lapse in an otherwise clean record. I decided that I should have to try to wear him down and that I should go back down to Mawlaik, make some enquiries and return to Homalin for another week.

A second week in Homalin was an agreeable prospect. I loved the atmosphere of quiet peaceful living there and was intrigued by my contacts with the elder Poo Nyo who was a fund of knowledge on the countryside and the animals and birds of the forest. At night I could hear the clamour of the greylag geese as they came in to the flooded land around us from far away north. I thought of their quite amazing flight from the cold wastes of Siberia down some Himalayan valley and why such great numbers of them should choose the Chindwin valley for their winter quarters. With some reluctance I allowed the elder Poo

Nyo to persuade me that I should "bag" one at least, when I returned. It was an opportunity that I might never have again.

When I returned to Mawlaik, Rattan Singh was not at all pleased that I was spending so much time dealing with this erring, part-time sub-Agent at Homalin. He warned me that the missing money could have been borrowed for my arrival there; and he did not have to tell me that news of my movements could well have preceeded me, for I knew already of the myterious ways in which word travelled in Burma. I was going to look foolish if Rattan Singh found Ba Tun with a shortage again and I had taken no action.

I decided to engage a *shey-ney,* which could be interpreted as a lawyer or simply a Court pleader. U San Pe was the latter and I took to him at once when I met him. I remember him well. About sixty-five years of age, slightly bent and with a gentle voice which had not one word of English to utter, he was the real old type of Burman with long hair twisted into a "bun" on top of his head and tied with a silk *gaung-baung*. He always wore a spotless white *eingyi* and a Mandalay silk *putsoe*.

I took U San Pe back up to Homalin with me, hoping that this appearance of pending Court proceedings would frighten Ba Tun into talking. For the next two weeks he was my constant companion and regaled me with tales of Burma in the time of the Burmese Kings which he remembered in his boyhood. He had welcomed British annexation and the peace it had brought, the justice and integrity of British administration and the prosperity which trade and communications had fostered. But he thought that the time must soon come when the British should return independence to Burma.

When we got to Homalin and I settled in at the dak bungalow for another week I hoped that this wise old man would prise something out of Ba Tun. But as the week wore on and the silence held we began to wonder if even Court proceedings would not be more trouble than it was all worth. It would be a flimsy case. U San Pe, however, kept the threat over the head of the unfortunate younger man and waited patiently.

As we lit our lamps on the last night of my second week in Homalin, the unmistakable sound of shoes being dropped from feet came from the wooden stair at the entrance to the dak bungalow. A young and well dressed Burman appeared and asked if he may come in. At once I recognised him as a police officer whom I had met on my first visit. I beckoned him to a chair. We had not called in the police and still had the next day to consider that, for we would join the steamer when she arrived the next evening. I wondered if he had come to offer help if we would disclose the purpose of our visit to Homalin. But no; he hesitated, then launched into a long explanation of his compulsive addiction to gambling and how he had persuaded his friend Ba Tun to lend him two hundred rupees to pay a debt which was about to land him in Court. Unfortunately for them, Rattan Singh had arrived unexpectedly in Homalin the next day and the mantle of trouble fell on Ko Ba Tun. By the time I arrived the police officer had won back sufficient to repay Ba Tun. They had kept hoping that I would forgive and forget but now he realised that if Ba Tun was taken to Court the whole story would have to come out and they would both be in trouble.

Here was a fine dilemma. While admiring Ba Tun's loyalty to his friend and with an immediate reaction that I should let him off with a warning, I was faced with another problem. I knew the District Superintendent of Police at Mawlaik, the man's superior officer, and would certainly be blameworthy if I did not report all this to him. I told the dejected police officer that this I must do and that he would have to hope for the best.

There could be no instant happy ending to this story. I forgave Ba Tun after giving him a lecture and made it clear that I was staking my own reputation on his own future good behaviour. The D.S.P. at Mawlaik sent for his erring officer and quite independently dealt out the same treatment; I hope that he had the same response as I did from Ko Ba Tun, for the Homalin sub-Agency was still his in 1942 when everything went by the board; and he was there and re-appointed in 1945 when the war was over and we sent steamers up the Chindwin again.

This cloud had hung over those otherwise pleasant weeks in Homalin as the weather became more and more like a fine English summer, but cold at nights with a fire welcome and several blankets in bed. Old Poo Nyo kept his promise and took me out to the countryside at five o'clock one morning to lie in wait beside a *jeel.* The geese would rise at dawn without fail, he said, and fly over our hide-out. They would be much faster in flight than they appeared and I was to shoot well ahead of the gaggle as they rose and came over us. I got my goose — but it was one of the last, a straggler which had lagged behind. I had to stand a good deal of Karen chaff thereafter. But if I was humble, I was also happy.

The coastline at the Mergui Archipelago.

SEVEN

WHERE THE SOUTH SEAS BEGIN

by Harold Braund

My story is titled from Morris Collis's description of Mergui and, to anyone who knew the place, it is apt. More specifically he wrote —

> "It is a town of some 20,000 inhabitants, situated on an island of the utmost fertility at the edge of a great archipelago. The inhabitants in general are dressed in Burmese clothes and use the language of that country, though they are of the mixed blood of Burma, Siam, Malaya, China and India, with strains of Portuguese and Arab. It is a place overshadowed by a various past."

In his 'Siamese White' Collis has chronicled the history of Mergui from the time in the seventeenth century when it was a Siamese port on the Bay of Bengal until it became a British possession two centuries later. It is a turbulent story, bound up with the history of The East India Company sailing out of Madras; a story of trading, marauding and warring. It is strange that after the dust and the clamour of that period had subsided so little has been written about Mergui.

On the other hand, perhaps, there is a reason for this. In the years leading up to the Second World War, Mergui had an odd irrelevance to the rest of Burma. It was rather akin to the human appendix, a bodily organ on which there is no dependence for survival by any other organ.

Apart from among a few civil servants and officers of The British India Steam Navigation Company there was little in the way of informed knowledge of the place elsewhere in Burma. There was minor trading intercourse with Rangoon in such activities as the shipment of *ngapi* (rotted fish) and mother-of-pearl products, but the bulk of Mergui's produce — all of the tin and most of the rubber — was carried southward to Penang. Of tourist traffic there was virtually none: the quality of Mergui's hostelry saw to that.

The traveller's only link with Rangoon was the B.I.'s 'Sir Harvey Adamson', a wallowing hulk which, having survived two world wars, turned turtle in a hurricane and went down with all on board trapped within her hull. No bodies or wreckage were ever found.

My memory of this particular ship's officers is of a breed apart, seemingly impervious or resistant to transfer. All seemed to have been with the ship for years. Perhaps the aura of Mergui wafted and influenced off-shore. Well remembered is the Chief Engineer. At the breakfast table he would argue heatedly the 'con' to your 'pro'. At dinner, with a little subtle manipulation on your part, he would argue your earlier 'pro' against his own self-same 'con' with no less vigour or sincerity. Well, these men are gone.

To the best of my knowledge, I was the only European mercantile Assistant — in living memory at least — ever to be posted to Mergui from a Rangoon head office. At Mergui there was nothing for the teak wallah; no paddy fields to attract the rice miller; no clangour from the rotary tables of wells drilling for oil. From Singapore and Penang there would be occasional staff postings to Mergui by tin and rubber companies having small-scale interests in Tenasserim. In all essential respects Mergui was Malaya-orientated. The Mergui Club was the only one in Burma where you asked for a *stengah* or a *pahit* when ordering a whisky or a gin.

Mergui's white population numbered about forty. This included outliers, myself among them, for whom travel to town involved a journey by launch — there being no roads — of up to several hours. Save for the few itinerants referred to, it was a static population — men sluicing for tin and a precarious living from the islands of *terra firma* among the mangrove: men squeezing rubber from acres of debilitated trees; and others from questionable pursuits, one of which may have been the prime factor in the disappearance of the rhinoceros from the Bilauktaung Range, which served the archipelago as a spine.

All these men were permanently rooted. For none was there the luxury of home leave, or the prospect of occasional transfer, or the rewards of advancing seniority, or the comfort of a rising bank balance as a cushion against the uncertainties of ultimate retirement or premature incapacity. They went nowhere: they married and bred locally: they scorned the papers and periodicals in the club in favour of the bar: they bent the law to the maximum: they acquired peculiarities of appearance and behaviour: they bore the stamp of the beachcomber: they were God's gift to Somerset Maugham.

Among this motley crew one stood out as a giant in any sense but the physical, though he was not a small man. Benjamin Jubb, eternally crop-headed, in singlet and *sarong* (it would have been a *longyi* elsewhere in Burma), feared neither God nor man; but men, at least, feared him. He was the best of company provided you never allowed yourself to forget that no slight, real or imagined; no attempt to 'put one over'; no advantage gained at his expense, however legitimately, ever went unrequited. With the Almighty he shared the dictum that 'Vengeance is Mine'. No matter how long it might take, retribution would come, often by a hand other than but guided by his own.

A trivial introduction, not involving retribution, for which there would have been no opportunity, but mentioned first because the incident occurred shortly before my arrival in Mergui, involved an officer of the R.A.F. With the clouds of war starting to gather, at least for those with eyes to see, Mergui harbour briefly was investigated as a base for flying boats engaged in costal surveillance. A Sunderland flying boat had touched down in the harbour. During the early evening the captain of the aircraft, later to be Air Vice-Marshal Cave-Brown-Cave, found his way to the as yet deserted Club. Smartly attired in hot weather rig, he was having a solitary drink at the bar when Jubb arrived on silent feet, clumped him on the back and invited him to join him.

With what must pardonably have been an undisguised look of distaste at such an uncouth apparition, the officer announced that 'I am Cave-Brown-Cave'. 'Oh, you are are you?' said Jubb, 'well I am Home-Sweet-Home' and he made his enraged exit. Oddly enough, while on leave some years later, I heard this story recounted in a railway carriage in England by someone having no connection with Mergui.

Jubb had a finger in every pie — tin mining and rubber planting to mention two of the sometimes more legitimate. Adjacent to a rubber plantation on which he had his dwelling, was a run-down plantation of no great acreage which Jubb decided he would like to add to his own domain. Having ascertained that the property was owned by a Roman Catholic Commission in Rangoon, Jubb wrote to them with a cash offer for it that included the 'chattels' on the plantation. The reply was to the effect that while the Commission was interested in selling, the terms on which the estate was held included a stipulation that it could only be sold to a Roman Catholic.

Jubb's religious persuasion, if any, could only be a matter for speculation; but it did emerge that he was not a Roman Catholic. However, the impediment presented no problem and Jubb took the steps necessary to acquire the requisite qualification.

There followed the drawing up of the deeds of sale, but progress became bogged down when the Commission protested against Jubb's understanding of the term 'chattels'. On the plantation was a domestic elephant, the value of which approximated to the total 'with chattels' price that Jubb had agreed to pay. Jubb maintained stoutly that the elephant was included in the sale price: the Commission riposted with a denial of any such intention.

Without involving himself in further protracted correspondence, Jubb fell back on another of his cardinal principles, which was that in a matter of this sort you should never deal with underlings. Accordingly he wrote direct to the Pope. The truth of the story I accept; but regretfully I never heard the outcome of this imaginative approach.

Another member of the beachcomber fraternity was a man I think it discreet to introduce as Bob Wood, because, on the death of his father, he would have become entitled to a seat in the House of Lords. Bob was a genuine remittance man. Whatever the shortcoming was that earned him expulsion from his manorial home, his exile was perpetuated by a regular sum of money payable only on condition that he remained at the other end of the earth. As it was, he managed a small rubber plantation whereon he lived with his Burmese wife and two children.

Bob was a harmless enough character to all outward seeming, but, somewhere along the line, he had crossed swords with Jubb and apparently bested him. It happened before my time and years had passed since the incident, whatever it may have been. While Jubb awaited his chance, I am sure that their relationship in the Club would have been outwardly cordial.

There came a day when Jubb surprised everybody by deciding to visit his native Yorkshire. In England, hair grown and suited in a manner that would have made him unrecognisable in Mergui, he called on Lady Wood (whose husband, I suspect, would have refused to have any part in a discussion involving his wayward son). After dilating upon the well-being of Bob back in the his *atap* shack, Jubb silkily deplored that so much of Lady Wood's generous allowance went on drink; and he persuaded her that some reduction would undoutedly have the effect of curtailing the scope for this damaging form of self-entertainment. My first reaction must be that the story is exaggerated if not apocryphal. But, as a line of escape, I must add that of no other character known to me is there such room for credibility. It fits Jubb to a T.

There came a day when, for the first time, the post of Deputy Commissioner, Mergui, was filled by other than a British official. With a facility that doubtless would have been lacking hitherto, Jubb manoeuvred the D.C. into a position of obligement to himself. He had the D.C.'s ear at all times. On hearing that the Governor of Burma was to make an official visit to Mergui, Jubb arranged with the D.C. that he and his wife would have a prominent role to play in the public reception.

Some days later the D.C., freshly primed by the Government House secretariat in Rangon, had the embarrassing duty of informing Jubb that he could not be included in the welcoming proceedings along with his wife because they were not lawfully married. Here, however, was another eventuality that had no place in the 'too hard' basket. Jubb staged a magnificent wedding, with the eldest of his six children as bridesmaid; and in his speech at the reception announced that after driving a car for twenty years he had decided to take out a licence.

Some years later I attended the wedding of that daughter-bridesmaid to the Australian Dredgemaster of a dredge operating further down the coast than my location. The best man was my Dredgemaster, also Australian, and he had asked me to escort his wife, a Chinese girl, to the Church and afterwards to the reception.

The line-up in the Sanctuary was Jubb on the left, then the bride and groom, then Danny Higgins the best man. Jubb had to be seen to be believed. His hair was still shaven to the skull, but he was attired almost certainly in the outfit he had had tailored for his his call on Lady Wood in England. Under his arm he nursed a coal-scuttle *topi* of such enormous size that it was always in danger of getting away from him.

We reached without disaster the point in the service where Jubb had to discharge the only duty required of him — presumably to answer 'I do' to the question 'Who gives this woman away?'.

This done, he solved the problem of the impatient *topi* by clapping it on his head. Muted mirth could be heard all round the Church but, to my alarm, Kim, the Chinese girl, burst into hysterical laughter and I had to cram a handkerchief into her mouth to quieten her down. Her outburst had aroused the congregation to greater mirth, and pandemonium was barely averted. Jubb, probably angry but all impassive, maintained his four-square stance in the Sanctuary, back to the congregation and *topi* squarely on his head. However undeservedly, it was the sort of thing that could have got *me* into his bad books but, fortunately, my days in Mergui were numbered by an Army Command soon to claim me for military service.

Jubb was well prepared for the Japanese invasion when it came. In the harbour he had his own small ocean-going schooner, fully provisioned, and he made it to the Seychelles with, I believe, all his family. He died there some years later. It had occurred to me, when contemplating the writing of these pages, to conceal his name. But I was deterred. If he has survived beyond the grave, I should have risked incurring his wrath. Jubb would reckon that he had nothing to hide.

Having said earlier that little has been written about twentieth century Mergui, my own pen picture of local characters requires mention that Maurice Collis himself wrote a novel based on prewar Mergui, where he had served three years as Deputy Commissioner. As a book it was at best a pot-boiler and, for some reason or other, Collis adopted the regrettable device of casting in an unpleasant role Mergui's most innocuous beachcomber. It was the sort of ploy more to be expected of Jubb.

Maxton Latour and his wife (I have disguised the name) belonged unmistakeably to the rooted element of Mergui's fraternity. They were, in my experience of them, a couple of the utmost integrity, for which reason, doubtless, they had succeeded in nothing that might lead to a bank balance. Without being destitute they were certainly impoverished, despite which there was always something offered in the way of home-baked goodies whenever I dropped in for a chat — which was something they welcomed. How they came to fetch up in Mergui I neither asked nor discovered. If there was a black mark somewhere it belonged, surely by this time, under the blanket of forgiveness.

Another of Mergui's wild men was a chap called Moisey; something of a 'loner', reputedly with soldiering in his past, and wholly unpredictable when in the clutches of alcohol. My own nearest neighbour, by great good fortune, was an ex-officer tin miner, George Wilson, one of the few already referred to as being on transfer from Malaya. Later he and I were to serve together, and he to die gallantly in the post-war Malayan 'emergency'.

One day when George and I had gone down to Mergui together, the Deputy Commissioner spotted us in the Club and asked us to go outside for a word with him. Moisey, he explained, had apparently gone off his rocker and was objecting by rifle fire to any attempt to approach his bungalow. He, the D.C., was reluctant to call in the police until he knew more about the situation and asked if we would be prepared to go and investigate since we both knew and were on good terms with Moisey. If an inference was to be drawn that we were regarded as more expendable than the D.C.'s few policemen, we did not argue it and set off for Moisey's rubber plantation some miles out of town. We both carried revolvers, since the object of our visit to Mergui was to collect cash for our respective pay rolls; and our destination and the tide table made the route and timing of our departure predictable.

When we arrived at Moisey's plantation, we spied out the land. His high-stilted bungalow was the centre point of a cleared circle of about a hundred yards radius. There was no sight or sound of Moisey. We repeatedly called his name, for if we could identify ourselves to his satisfaction we felt there would be no need to risk heroics. There was no response.

We set off, running alternately in short stretches, the one covering the other while he was on the move. We reached the steps, about twenty of them, and raced to the top. We found Moisey flat on his back, dead drunk. We brought him round by violently slapping and pummelling him and got some food into him. Of his recent behaviour he had no recollection at all and was most contrite. We deemed it impolitic to ask for the drinks we so badly needed and left after assuring ourselves, more or less, that he would cause no further trouble.

Moisey's immense front room, open on three sides, I will always remember. It comprised more than half the total floor space of the bungalow. It alone was furnished, and that to the extent of a bed, a table and a chair, an arsenal of shot guns and rifles, and hanging on the only wall an immense family tree tracing his own descent from Sir Richard de Maisey, who invaded England in the entourage of William the Conqueror!

In 'Distinctly I Remember' I have recorded that after my departure from Mergui —

> "Moisey and Danny Higgins, whether with or without military enrolment and in what circumstances I have never been able to learn, joined some sort of armed foray from Mergui into Siam from which none returned."

Over thirty years later I received a telephone call in Melbourne from a man who introduced himself as a retired geologist from Malaya. Having just read my book, he thought I would be interested to learn that both Moisey and Higgins had shared his internment in a civilian prison camp in Siam and that both had survived to be freed at the end of the war. Perhaps, after all, the foray was just a drunken spree? If so, at least they had three years in which to sober up!

Gladly would I have gone back to Mergui for a spell after the war, but the opportunity was never there. Now, after all these years, the beauty of the place will remain — the countless islands with their exquisite sandy beaches, the miles of waterways fracturing the mangrove swamp, the concourse of craft both ocean-going and riverine, the phosphorescence in the water, the myriad fireflies busying themselves along the banks, the 'plop' of a startled crocodile sliding into the water from its mud bank. Yes, all these will be as before.

What will have gone is 'my' generation of beachcombers. They were all older men than myself and, even if they survived the Japanese occupation, their bones by now will have been laid to rest. The nationalistic status of Burma will have ensured that no new generation of such characters crouches beside the sluices or taps for rubber. Perhaps a few old shades will foregather in the Club (whatever its present role) on evenings when the ghostly outlines of 'Sir Harvey Adamson' ride at anchor in the harbour. Perhaps and perhaps. *Eheu fugaces!*

H.E.W. BRAUND, M.B.E., M.C.

Harold Braund is the author of two notable books. His autobiographical account of his years in Burma from 1934 to 1946 earned him election to the fellowship of Australian Writers. He also compiled a history of the first hundred years of Steel Brothers and Company (1870-1970).

Harold is of Devon ancestry. He was born in Ceylon (now Sri Lanka) in 1913 and the call of the East led him to Steels when his education in England was complete. They sent him to Burma and made him an oil man. This took him to the oilfields, including the remote field of Indaw in Upper Chindwin, a posting only for men of more than ordinary stamina. Later, before his release in 1940 to Army service, he spent two years in the Tenasserim Archipelago that forms Burma's long "kite tail". There, some way south of Mergui, Steels had a tin dredging enterprise and encounters with beachcombers were commonplace. It was real Somerset Maugham country.

Commissioned in the Burma Frontier Force he spent three years of the Japanese war operating with levies in the Chin Hills and was awarded the Military Cross and mentioned in despatches.

Steels sent him to their Attock Oil Company in Pakistan after the war. He was General Manager when he completed his service for them there in 1965, having been awarded the M.B.E. for services to the British community. He then settled in Australia with his family and has recently retired to a corner of New South Wales called Coff's Harbour, appropriately named for a man who has led such a nomadic life. There he practises as a "small time" writer of light verse.

EIGHT

SMALL TALES OF A HILL BILLY

by Noel Stevenson

Spreading the tiger skin on my lawn the elders started to tell their story in the usual circumlocutory manner of the mountain men, filling in the background before disclosing what it was all about. "Our tiny village of five houses," they began, prompting and interrupting each other as the tale unfolded, "had barely come to life because, as you know *Duwa,* it's the season of leisure between the harvest and cutting the jungle for next year's crops. The ridge on which the village stands is narrow and steep-sided and it slopes sharply down to the west so that the houses sit like the steps of a stair, each on its little platform of bare earth overlooking those below. The houses themselves are small and poor, and the sun-bleached thatch with patches of *shingbwi* palm leaf will tell you that all the young men are away, some in the Army, some cane-cutting in the plains and one or two off to buy opium over the border in Yunnan. Well, when all this happened the old men were sunning themselves as usual in their front porches, doing odd jobs like splitting firewood or bamboo to make *chingkhyen* for the house floors. Our womenfolk were sitting in a little group gossiping and watching a young girl weaving her first *pachyet* kerchief for her lover while the children played around them. Near the lowest house a little girl of seven was trying her hand at spinning with a spindle nearly as long as her arm. All was very quiet and peaceful and drowsy.

"Suddenly there was a flash of tawny yellow from the jungle edge and a wild scream from the little spinner. A full grown young tiger stood over her, its jaws gripping her shoulders. As the womenfolk shrieked in terror and grabbed their infants the child's father rushed from his porch, sword in hand, and fell upon the tiger. His blade slashed into neck and shoulder but the tiger struck out with its forepaw at the hapless man's face, tearing it apart. Dropping the child, it stood snarling over the body of her dead father. Meanwhile the old widower from the house above had also gone running to the rescue, cursing and waving his light sword. He too had a slash at the tiger's head but missed and was felled unconscious by a massive swipe which raked his body with inch-deep claw cuts. The tiger was still standing roaring over its victim when our headman, reacting to the cries of "Sharaw! Sharaw!", picked up a heavy Burmese *dah* and ran down to help. By then the striped demon had had enough of interference and charged to meet him. In a move of wild despair the headman brought his *dah* down two-handed as the beast bowled him over, striking it fair between the eyes. He rolled over and jumped to his feet, expecting to be charged again, but his blow had split the tiger's skull and it lay quivering and dying where it fell. We soon finished it off. Now we've brought the skin to claim the Rs. 40/- official bounty."

As I listened to them in admiration I was thinking, "It's easy to understand the father's reaction and even that of the old widower, as he was the girl's uncle. But the headman? Did Kachin *noblesse oblige* alone account for his suicidal courage? Or was he just a "bonny fechter" anxious to prove a point?" I suddenly realised that in all the excitement of the tale I had not yet asked which of them was the ultimate hero of the contest — the headman himself. They pointed to a man sitting by the head of the skin, fingering a long gash in it. He was about five feet one or two, thin as a rake and with a great gnarled goitre half hidden under his straggly grey beard. I could only marvel. Rarely can such supreme contempt for danger have been packaged in so inconspicuous a frame. Their faces fell when I had to tell them that the Government had abandoned the bounty system as too many tigers were being killed, but they cheered up when I told them that we in Sinlumkaba would club together to buy them a flintlock gun so that they would be better able to protect themselves in future.

* * *

Suzanna was a pig, an English Large Black to be precise, bred at the American Baptist Mission farm at Pyinmana in Central Burma. Little did she realise as she lay in her comfortable pen that in the years to come her distant descendants would be among the few remaining traces of British rule left in the Kachin Hills. While stationed at Sinlumkaba I had promised the tribal chiefs that I would give them a porcine matriarch which would mother a new generation of pigs to put the local razor-backs to shame and give their people a chance to cut in on the trade in pigs-on-the-hoof which passed through their villages from Yunnan to Bhamo. She would be kept at the boarding school at

Sinlumkaba and her male progeny would be given to the best scholars to take back to their villages. With starry-eyed optimism I saw myself as the founder of a genetic revolution whose name would ring through Kachin history every time a pig was sacrificed to the tribal gods.

So, in due course, Miggie and I stopped off at Pyinmana on our way back from short leave in Rangoon to choose our prize. The Berkshire pigs on display were rejected summarily, as a previous experiment in the Chin Hills had foundered on their white spots. All Chin pigs were sacrificed to the household spirits before being eaten, and the spirits would accept none with white markings. The kindly soldier who had donated the animals ended up having to eat his gifts himself. Then we saw Suzanna, gorgeously black, enormous at the best of times but now monstrous in pregnancy, and closed the deal at once.

We had to catch the north-bound mail train next morning at the grisly hour of 3 a.m. and it took a platoon of sleepy porters to heft her massive crate into the guard's van, where she settled down complacently for her sixteen hour journey in the heat. We sluiced her down at every station and fed her as best we could on the produce of the platforms, mainly bananas and hard boiled eggs which she ate skins and shells and all. Darkness had fallen by the time we reached the railhead at Katha, where a gang of Burmese porters carried her smartly on to the deck of the Irrawaddy Flotilla steamer which was to take us upstream to Bhamo, dumping her in a quiet corner where I hoped she would remain undisturbed.

I had not realised I had brought a time-bomb aboard, for the entire crew was Muslim. When a passing crewman asked me "Is that a bear you have in there, Sahib?" I replied in all innocence "No, it's a pedigree sow I'm taking up to the Sinlum hills." The man leapt back as if he's seen a ghost and let out a wild scream for the Serang, who came a-running, stared in disbelief, and started to call down all manner of damnations on the villains who had brought the pig aboard. When he discovered that I was the villain he tried desperately to control his wrath, ordering me between clenched teeth to get the pig off the boat at once. "We are all Muslims, Sahib," he cried. "We cannot sail with a pig on board. We have an agreement with the Company that we will never have to carry pigs." I pointed out that all the Burmese porters had gone home to bed and that if he wanted the pig unloaded he and his crew would have to do it.

The argument warmed up. He cried to Allah that pigs were excreta-eaters and hopelessly polluted and that his men would never touch the crate. I swore that Suzanna was as pollution-free as driven snow, that she had never been out of a pen, never eaten anything that he would not eat himself. He turned a deaf ear. Buoyed by the pride of Islam and the backing of the Company's rule he shouted angrily, "If you do not take the pig off we shall not sail. If I take it to Bhamo the hundreds of Muslims in Bhamo would want to cut my throat." "Right," I snarled, "If that's what you fear let me tell you that there are fifty thousand tough Kachins in the hills just waiting for this pig and if you do not sail, then, by the Lord Harry, I'll lead them down myself to extirpate the lot of you!" For a moment there was deadlock. Mahomet had come face to face with the mountain.

The Serang departed suddenly to his cabin and returned in his best uniform, the better to outface me. It was his undoing, for I saw he was wearing his World War I medal ribbons and I had a happy thought. "Ah!" I said sneakily, "I see you are an old warrior." "In truth Sahib," he said proudly, swelling his chest, "I was even on the first boat to relieve Kut-al-Amara." I had him. "Then by Heaven," I thundered, "You are a hypocrite and a rascal. Did you not carry pork and beans to Kut? And bacon and other unmentionables? How dare you then deny this porcine princess a passage?" "But Sahib," he protested, "That was war!" "And by the Prophet this will be war if we do not sail at once," I countered. He began to waver under this unexpected attack and I followed up quickly, "If we go without delay and you do not blow your siren till after the ship is tied up at Bhamo we can get the pig ashore and out of sight before anyone arrives." He hesitated, then gave way at last, on two conditions. The first was that I must sign a note to guarantee that the Government would not use the incident as a precedent to start a pig trade down the river. The second was that Suzanna should travel in the ladies lavatory, Third Class.

In her crate she journeyed up the six thousand feet to Sinlumkaba like a great beetle held aloft by a multitude of ants, to become the hottest tourist attraction the hills had ever known. The schoolboys built a beautiful little house for her in the school orchard, where she lived in pampered luxury. The wily headmaster Maran La soon realised her entertainment value and charged a pice apiece from the scores who wanted to see her every bazaar day. When her sprightly piglets arrived visiting numbers soared and we were soon in a position to arrange her marriage out of peepshow funds. Not wanting to start a *jihad,* we had the Large Black boar sent up by the long tortuous land routes through the Shan States, only to discover on his arrival that he was too huge to mate with even the biggest of village sows. All would have to depend on the male progeny of his monogamous life with Suzanna, and it was clear that they would have to be distributed for stud while they were still young enough to catch their nimble mountain mates.

Suzanna's nuptials were almost a total failure. The boar proved to be a hopeless marksman and deposited his seed everywhere except where it was needed. In desperation, and inspired by a hundred eager onlookers, we seized and held the brute by main force while the headmaster steered him in the right direction. This time we were successful. Suzanna looked coyly appreciative and the ribald Kachins gave the headmaster and myself joint credit for the fatherhood of her next lively litter. My place in Kachin history was assured!

* * *

There was no doubt about it. I was in a bad temper and it showed. I had snapped at my bearer because he had not had dry clothes ready the instant I arrived at my camp. I had snapped at the cook because the excellent dinner he had prepared was not what I felt like eating that particular evening. I had bawled at the headman and his elders in a most unseemly manner, sending them off sad and crestfallen. Worst of all I had even refused the request of the village children to play my gramophone for them after dinner. All this because one of my mules had been injured slightly falling through a bridge the villagers were supposed to have repaired. Keeping the village tracks open for mules was the only task the Government imposed on the villagers of these remote northern hills, and one day's work a year was usually enough for the job. I felt I had good reason for displeasure.

The rain had stopped. The children were still hanging around in little groups hoping against hope that I would change my mind. Their squeaks and whispers stung my conscience, for after all the fault was not theirs, but I hardened my heart and prepared for bed. At last they drifted off in twos and threes and in the still night air I could hear their cries of disappointment as they complained to their mothers about the hard-hearted *Duwa* who took his anger out on them. Before long the strident voices of the womenfolk could be heard berating their men for creating all the trouble and soon the air was crackling with acrimony as the rows developed. The owner of the nearest house raised his voice in anger to shout in despair, "All right then. What d'you expect me to do? Go out and mend the accursed bridge at this time of night?" "Why not?" shrilled his wife, "You layabouts started all this. Why can't you get torches and do something about it?" Silence fell as the husband digested this bit of advice, and I heard the *chingkhyen* flooring creaking as he went off grumbling into the night. Half an hour later a rumble of voices roused me as a string of men bearing torches disappeared down the way I had come. "Serve the lazy blighters right," I thought, "Their wives have more muscle than the Government!"

I went off to sleep, sure that by the time they had walked to the bridge and repaired it my bearer would be waking me for the next day's march. I should have known better. In what seemed an impossibly short time I was awaked by a susurration of whispers and coughs and spits to find my tent glowing in the light of dozens of torches. Struggling into some clothes I found the headman and his elders assembled outside, stirring up the embers of the fire and looking as if they were prepared to spend the rest of the night there. When he saw me emerge the headman jumped to his feet crying, "We have repaired the bridge, *Duwa,* now you can play the gramophone. The children are all waiting." Surveying the serried ranks behind him, I knew I was beaten. I had had my pound of flesh and now they wanted theirs. Lost sleep seemed a small price to pay for all the midnight effort to please their youngsters, so I spun the old HMV portable until dawn was breaking.

My own unexpected reward was out of all proportion to my sacrifice. As a spin-off from the night's work I found I had uncovered an administrative weapon of unqiue power. After that night I knew I had only to say, "Right, no gramophone!" and I could move mountains.

* * *

The Putao subdivision, with its headquarters at Fort Hertz, is the northernmost corner of Burma. In my time there it was twenty-one days march by jungle mule-track from the railhead at Myitkyina, sparsely populated and with vast areas of uninhabited jungle stretching to the Tibetan border. It was a wild and improbable place where improbable things happened of a kind beyond the imagination of plains-dwellers.

For example, when I first arrived there in 1930 I found Fort Hertz overflowing with nubile Nung girls just down from the distant fastnesses of the Nam Tamai in search of their menfolk. Earlier in the year Captain Jimmy Green of the Burma Rifles had been there on a highly successful recruiting tour and dozens of strapping young Nungs had followed him down to Myitkyina to join the army or find work cane-cutting at Sahmaw. The girls had been dismayed to find on reaching Fort Hertz — to them the centre of civilisation — that they were still far far away from their husbands and lovers. "Where shall we get children?" they cried, "When our men are all away?" There were some dozens of wifeless and ardent young Gurkha soldiers in the post so it was with some haste that I gave each of the girls a week's rations and packed them off home under the guard of two of my Nung policemen. The latter returned a fortnight later looking rather wan.

Some weeks later I went on the annual tour to their homeland on the eastern border with Yunnan, truly a dream march into the halls of the mountain gods. The giant trenches of the Nam Tamai and the Taron Kha are thousands of feet deep, the roaring waters so far below the scattered villages that they cannot be heard, though the people sing to each other across the void. Five days march took me to the rickety bridge over the Nam Tamai, the beginning of the country of the Nungs and Lisus, and from then on our journey became a carnival. Whole villages of men, women and children accompanied us along, chattering and laughing and singing songs across the river. By night it was all revelry, Nungs and Lisus vying with each other to demonstrate their dances to the music of drums, gourd pipes and a ukulele-like guitar. Little work was done. Men who had nursed grievances for months against the coming of the *Duwa* found themselves easily persuaded by their fellows that it would be too bad to spoil the fun by argument. I dare say many agreements made were subsequently regretted, but they were made, and once made, accepted.

My most important task was to pay for the upkeep of the mule tracks and collect the small annual house-tax of one rupee. The whole process was an elaborate charade to establish our suzerainty. A tax is a normal symbol of overlordship. But taxes cannot be paid where there is no money, so the routine of first paying for the mule tracks was established so that the civil officer could pay out enough going in one direction to be able to collect house tax on the return journey. The two sums never matched and each year a little more money was left behind.

One night, when I was gossiping with the elders, a retired havildar of the Burma Rifles made an impassioned appeal for a school for the Nung country. At the time there was not a single school north of Myikyina. The budget for the district covered only keeping the peace and no thought had ever been given to improving the condition of the hillmen. I told the havildar that I was trying to persuade the American Baptist Mission to start a school near Putao and that was the best I could hope for. The elders nodded sleepily and changed the subject, but other sharp ears had recorded it.

Four days march after we had left for home I went off to shoot a pheasant for my supper and came upon nearly seventy Nung children camped by a stream. Lured by my tale of a possible school they had tagged along behind my party, scared to let me discover their presence, sleeping huddled together in the jungle, uncovered and unprotected. We soon found that they had not told their parents either. We could not spare the time to escort them home again nor risk sending them back alone, and anyway their courage and enterprise deserved a better fate, so I took them along with me like the Pied Piper of Hamelin. There was a happy ending for their story touched the hearts at district headquarters and we got the money for two teachers. A school was soon established, local chiefs putting up the buildings and providing food for the boarders. A first generation of educated Nungs was on its way.

NINE

THE DISCHARGE

by "Tawtha"

For many years it was my lot to live in the teak forests of Burma, from where so much of our fine shipbuilding timber came; it was my job to fell and drag the teak trees down to the rivers and to launch the logs into the channel where they would await the spate which would ultimately carry them down to the sawmills in Rangoon.

The usual method of moving the logs on their journey was to drag them by elephant and in those days each firm owned or hired large numbers of elephants for this work. Some of these, nearly always males, were of uncertain temper and a few were real bad 'uns which took any chance they could to kill their attendants or anyone else who was unwary enough to come within range of their tusks or trunk. The *oozie* (rider) or his assistant was nearly always the victim, for no matter how experienced a man was or how careful he was to start with, familiarity seemed inevitably to breed contempt.

That at least was how if often looked when a case was investigated, but it is only fair to add that the elephant had all the odds on his side, the initiative always lay with him. Whether he felt well disposed or in the worst of tempers, only a very experienced and wide-awake man could tell, and it is — as any soldier will tell you — impossible to be on the *qui vive* every day and all day.

These "killers" were released each evening along with the other animals, the practice being to shackle the forelegs loosely so that the animal could slowly make its way into the jungle and forage for itself. In the morning the *oozies* followed up the trail and having located their animal they unshackled the fetters and drove it back to camp to be harnessed for work. It was the unshackling that was the most dangerous part of the *oozie's* day.

In the case of a known killer there were supposed to be two men on the job, but even if there were they were almost certainly out of earshot of any assistance. It seems a fair assumption,

Two male elephants (tuskers). Shortly after this photograph was taken the one on the left killed his *oozie*. The wooden bell hanging from his neck was then changed to a killer's brass bell.

Tusker dragging a teak log.

moreover, that no animal, elephant or other, relishes being recalled to work in like circumstances in the morning. One has only to remember the average human reaction to realise the force of this; a morning liver is by no means confined to the *genus homo,* and the more elderly and autocratic the animal concerned, the more likely was he to resent that "damned fellow back again".

What most frequently happened was that one or other of the attendants fell sick and the other went out by himself, confident that what he had done for the the last few months, with a mate, could be done this morning without one. He usually got away with it, but perhaps he didn't, depending on the killer's liver. If it was his unlucky day, the first realisation of anything being wrong would be his non-arrival back in camp. The headman in charge would then order a party to investigate and generally it was not long till the body was found. Occasionally the man would be still alive, but I cannot recall a single case when an attendant got away merely with wounds. If a blow, whether it was from tusk, trunk or foot, caught a man squarely then he required no more, though he might live for a few hours.

The work of the whole camp was suspended until the funeral ceremony was over, but as a rule this was a simple affair in jungle. One of the requisites, however, was a formal discharge from service by the employer of the dead man, in this case the Assistant in charge of the area concerned.

I remember the first time I was asked for this formal letter of discharge addressed to the dead man personally. I was somewhat taken aback and asked the headman if it was really necessary. The strength of his reply, backed up even more strongly by the wife of the deceased man, convinced me that it was a very serious matter to them. Accordingly, I wrote out a letter to the man informing him that, as from the date of his death, there was no more work for him and that his services were accordingly terminated. This was carefully taken away by the wife for the purpose of showing it to the spirit of the deceased, who I was assured would otherwise hang about the camp in a way that would be embarrassing to the others. To make quite certain that the dead man saw his notice to quit, it was finally pinned down on his grave in such a way that only a very active or deliberately obtuse spirit could possibly miss it when taking his departure.

Only once do I remember the discharge being refused. The

Company knew nothing of it at the time, but the Assistant concerned was drinking a bit too much and acting so queerly that it was thought that he was being drugged. He was a man of about ten years service whom I shall call M., retiring and reticent to an unusual degree, and I would never have heard of the incident had I not happened to engage his servant some years later, when M. had left the service and the country. Maung Yon proved to be a sound and reliable servant and during his period of service with me I never had any reason to doubt his veracity.

Maung Yon had been with me for about a year when one of our most dangerous beasts killed his *oozie*. He was a mean and cunning tusker called Pu Kaw. It so happened that I was very busy at the time, on the point of moving camp to another quite distant part of the area. I had to go and inspect the corpse and make the usual enquiries, but I had previously given orders for the camp to be struck and the move to be made. The headman had accompanied me during the inspection and enquiry and at the conclusion he asked me for the usual discharge. I had forgotten my notebook that morning and no paper was immediately available in the camp, so I rather brusquely told him that I would give the certificate on my return in about two weeks' time. He said nothing more but I could not fail to see that he gave me a very peculiar sort of look, and I noticed him saying a few hurried words to the man who was guiding me to the new camp.

I thought nothing of this at the time, but on arrival there I saw this man in long and earnest conversation with Maung Yon. Inevitably the tragedy kept intruding itself into my thoughts and I had to consider the effect it might have on the rest of the labour force; but I had my report to write and there was also the urgent question of finding a new *oozie* who was willing for a few extra rupees to risk his neck with an animal now reputed to have raised his score to seven. Yet there was in my mind a vaguely uneasy feeling that something was wrong.

That evening when the office work was all done Maung Yon brought me my usual peg of whisky before dinner. Then he suddenly squatted down in front of me and asked permission to speak. Without more ado he referred to the death of the *oozie* and asked if it was true that I had refused to give a discharge. At once I replied that this was not so; all I had done was say that I would give it on my return in two weeks' time. His discomfiture was immediately apparent and I rather stupidly remarked that if the spirit of the deceased was as slack as the man himself had been, two weeks would be neither here nor there. At this Maung Yon's ugly brown face positively became several shades paler. Fear and horror were there too and I could almost hear him shiver. But after a moment or two, during which he managed successfully to convey a sense of wind-up to me, he pulled himself together.

"Thakin, Thakin" he said in tones of insistent urgency, "you must not delay. The man who accompanied you today still waits, and tonight, now, you must write the certificate so that he can take it back at once."

"But why all this hurry, Maung Yon" I replied. "I have never intended to refuse the discharge and surely a few days doesn't really matter."

Maung Yon at this laid his hand on my foot, which in those days a servant would not do except in very unusual circumstances.

"Thakin" he said, "do you remember M. *Thakin?* Do you remember when he was stationed in the north area and he went so queer that everyone thought he was drugged? I was his *lugale* at the time as you know and he was not drugged. No, he wasn't drugged, but" and here Maung Yon's voice fell to a whisper, *"he refused to give a discharge*. You remember the case, *Thakin*. I can see it in your face; you must believe me. I was with him and I saw what he saw. You must write the discharge now and give it to the man who waits. If you will do that I shall tell you the story of M. *Thakin*. But I beseech you first to write the discharge."

By this time I was definitely upset by Maung Yon's obvious wind-up and since the man to carry the letter was still here and paper and ink were now to hand, there seemed no good reason to delay any longer. Without further ado I therefore wrote out in the native script a letter to the deceased on the usual lines and signed it on behalf of the Company. The relief on Maung Yon's face was beyond doubt and he could hardly wait for an envelope before calling up the messenger. The latter clearly was aware of the situation and needed no instructions as to the destination of the letter. He disappeared into the darkness without paying any heed to a last minute injunction by Maung Yon to hurry.

Maung Yon had by now recovered a good deal of his composure and again squatted down beside my chair.

"Thakin" he said, "I am going to tell you this story because I

have said I will tell it, but none of the other *Thakins* have heard it and I beg of you not to repeat it unless for the same purpose that I tell it to you tonight. You will find it difficult to believe that I saw what I saw, but I swear to it and M. *Thakin* saw the same thing. I promised to tell you it because I feared you might continue to refuse the discharge and that we might see the same as M. *Thakin* and I saw."

Here Maung Yon gave a perceptible shiver.

"You remember that notorious killer Nga Kywe who had killed at least five men" he went on. "We were camped on the upper reaches of the Little Red River that December when Nga Kywe killed his *oozie* and bolted into the jungle. I knew that it was a bad killing from the talk about the camp and the men who saw the corpse said that Nga Kywe must have gored him first. There was a large hole through one of his thighs and his right arm was torn off at the shoulder."

I checked Maung Yon with my hand, for I wanted to hear no more of the gory details. I knew only too well what some of these killers did if they went berserk after the killing.

"It is enough, *Thakin,* I need not tell you more about the body, but I want you to remember what I have told you. The reason you will see later. It was afternoon when the headman came to tell M. *Thakin* and ask him to come and see the body. The headman told him what the corpse looked like and I could see that he had no wish to go at all but knew there was no alternative. As it was, he had been drinking more than was good for him at the time and his nerves were not good. Before he went off he called and made me bring him a big tot of whisky.

"It was after dusk when they returned and M. *Thakin* was looking and obviously feeling ill. He called for more whisky and instead of letting me pour it out for him as usual he took the bottle and poured himself half a glass, which he swallowed in two or three gulps. He then ordered the headman to wait and called me to bring his bath. After he had changed I could see that he was in a bad temper, not unusual for him when he had several drinks. He had another and I then reminded him that the headman was still waiting to see him.

"'Damn the b - - - - -, it's all his bloody fault' he shouted. Then he thought a minute and told me to call the headman up. There was no need for me to warn him of M. *Thakin's* temper. He could hear every word that had been said and had seen him take the whisky.

"There is no call for me to tell you all that was said between them. I think the headman had been slack in allowing the *oozie* to go out alone to bring in Nga Kywe when everyone in the camp knew that the elephant was in a period of particularly vicious temper. Anyhow, as the talk went on, M. *Thakin* grew more angry and finally threatened to sack the headman. I don't think he meant it but he certainly was in a foul temper and in the end told the man to go back to his camp and get all his animals back at work the next day without fail. I was taken aback at this, because I knew that they had not had time to bury the corpse and I was sure there would be trouble with the other *oozies* if the usual customs were not observed.

"The headman pointed this out and asked for the dead man's discharge certificate. It was the last straw. M. *Thakin* lost control of himself completely, jumped up and cursed the dead *oozie,* cursed the headman and told him to get to hell out of it before he came and made *him* look like the corpse. The man rapidly went down the steps of the hut and from the darkness outside he shouted that was not going to work under M. *Thakin* any longer and that the *Thakin* would bitterly regret what he had done. The *Thakin* slumped back into his chair and called for more whisky.

"About nine o'clock I tried to tell him that it was past dinner time but he just waved me away. I watched him for a while and he then seemed to fall asleep and I must have fallen asleep myself. It must have been some time later that I became conscious again, for when I opened my eyes the lamp had burned low and I began to trim it before making another attempt to get the *Thakin* to eat or at least to bed.

"As I was trimming the lamp I suddenly realised what had wakened me. It was the sound of Nga Kywe's bell. There was no mistaking it, for he wore a special brass killer's bell and we all knew its note. It was still some distance away but I could hear it coming steadily nearer and it was easy to tell by the note that it was being ridden and not merely on its own. I went to tell M. *Thakin,* but there was no need. He too had heard it and was sitting up, apparently sober and listening intently.

"'Maung Yon, Maung Yon', he called when he saw me, 'they must have recaptured Nga Kywe, but why are they bringing him here at this time of night?' I could see that he was puzzled and also apprehensive, for I think that the last words of the headman were still on his mind. I was also puzzled, for I could think of no good reason for the men to bring Nga Kywe along to our camp so late at night. I was also thinking that they must have brought him a long way. As the bell came steadily nearer, kling klang, kling, klang, kling klang, I began to feel a queer sinking feeling in my stomach. I swear that I had no inkling of what was coming, but there was something about the notes of that bell, remorselessly drawing nearer, which made me want to run away. By now we could hear the clink clink of Nga Kywe's chains mingled with the kling klang of the bell, then the occasional snort and snuffle that an elephant makes on the march. M. *Thakin* was now sitting bolt upright listening intently, and peering into the darkness.

"When it sounded as if the elephant was about fifty yards away, the clink clink of the chains suddenly ceased. The bell gave a jangle and then went silent too. *Thakin,* you know that these are the sounds of an elephant on the march stopping. But there was one thing unusual and that was the absence of a word of command from whoever was riding. I don't think this struck me at once, for although a spoken command is usual it is, as you know, not necessary to give it. What was striking me was that there was no sound of men accompanying and no lights, as they would surely have brought at that time of night. There was just dead silence, broken by a soft snuffle from Nga Kywe. I felt I wanted nothing more than to run down the back steps of the hut.

"Then I saw M. *Thakin* suddenly turn his head towards me as if to speak and then we both heard together another sound, an indescribable shuffle, of something coming towards the foot of the steps. It wasn't Nga Kywe, of that I felt sure. It was a far lighter, softer sound, almost like a sack might make being drawn along in irregular jerks. M. *Thakin* turned his head again towards the head of the steps. I think he knew by then what was coming, but he clearly had no control over his limbs, as indeed I had none. Slowly and inexorably the shuffle started to mount the steps, the top of a spear appeared, and *then* . . . ."

Maung Yon stopped, shivered and then went on in a whisper. "*Thakin,* you may believe it or not, but I swear as I am here tonight, *it was Nga Kywe's oozie!*

"I have told you already what the corpse looked like. There was no possible mistake. Its thigh had an enormous gash in it which was still oozing blood, its right arm was missing and the head was twisted round as if the neck had been broken, as it had been as I discovered later. The eyes were nearly closed and the face and body were half covered with blood, still wet. It had no clothes but still grasped in the left hand a big elephant spear with the shaft broken.

"This ghastly *thing* reached the top of the steps with its slow, laborious shuffle and then stopped. There was dead silence for what seemed like minutes. I tried to shout but no sound came. I tried to turn but my limbs were frozen. My eyes were glued to the awful sight. Then I saw M. *Thakin* suddenly jerk to his feet; with a horrible high pitched scream he picked up the tumbler which was by his hand and hurling it at the *thing* he staggered and fell.

"As he fell he knocked over the oil lamp on the table by his side. At that I came to life again and am not ashamed to tell you that I ran to the back of the hut and jumped clean over the verandah on to the ground, where I fell in a heap and half fainted with a twisted ankle. As I lay there, I heard as though in a dream the sudden jangle of a brass bell, then the clink clink of chains and the shuffle of an elephant's feet. It took some seconds to realise that it was Nga Kywe's bell and that he was going away.

"I lay listening to the steadily retreating kling klang of the bell; slowly, my senses and perhaps my courage began to come back to me. A hurricane lamp was still alight in the back part of the hut where I kept the dishes and cooking utensils. From where I lay I could hear nothing and see nothing, but I smelt kerosene from the upturned table lamp and feared that the wick might be smouldering enough to set fire to the kerosene soaked bamboo floor. I called out to the *Thakin* but there was no reply. I called again, this time to the other servants who were sleeping in another hut some twenty yards away, but my call brought no reply. I knew then that they had heard the bell and the scream and had bolted into the forest.

"I smelt the kerosene again. I tried my ankle and found that I could stand again, though painfully. With my heart in my mouth I slowly crept up the back steps and looked through the mat wall. The light penetrated only dimly but it was sufficient to see that M. *Thakin* was not lying there!

"*Thakin,* I can't tell you why, but I knew that the *thing* had gone with Nga Kywe and though I still feared greatly I was able to get the hurricane lamp and force myself to go into the front part of the hut. There lay the lamp in a pool of kerosene but nothing else except that the pool extended towards the top of the steps as if something had been dragged through it in that direction. As I came near this spot I saw bits of the broken tumbler. I was staring at these when I heard a sound which made my heart nearly stop. It was a groan and seemed to come from the bottom of the steps. Again it came and I recognised it as the *Thakin's* voice. I held the lamp high and saw him lying at the foot of the steps. His face was covered with blood and he was trying to struggle to sit up. That was bad enough, but nothing to the cold fear that descended again on me when I saw that *the steps were also covered with blood!* I remembered the awful wounds of the *thing* and had not M. *Thakin* groaned again I think I would have run away there and then.

"I was still trying to collect myself when I heard one of the other men calling and when I called back he answered. You can imagine my relief when a minute later I saw the light of a hurricane lamp approaching and heard voices. It was two of our *oozies* and another of our men. They had heard Nga Kywe and then M. *Thakin's* scream and were frightened, but not scared; of the *thing* they knew nothing. I did not mention it but asked them to help me carry the *Thakin* into the hut. I told them he was drunk and had fallen down the steps, which they believed readily enough. He had come round by this time but was dazed and gave no indication of remembering what had happened.

"There is not much more to tell, *Thakin.* We helped him to bed and in the morning when he wakened I brought him a cup of tea. I could tell at once from the look he gave me that he remembered. He was looking very white and ill, but he struggled to get up and made me bring a pen and paper. When I did so he told me to write an order to Nga Kywe's *oozie* informing him that he was discharged from that day. I saw here a chance to test if M. *Thakin* really remembered what had passed and told him that the discharge should date from the previous day, the day of the man's death.

"'Maung Yon' he said, 'you know as I know that he was not discharged yesterday. *He knows too!* He only came because I said yesterday that I would not release him. Write as I tell you and order a man to stand by to take the letter at once to the headman.'

"I did as I was bidden and he signed in a very shaky hand. He lay in bed that day and by evening he had a high fever. Some days later he sent a message to headquarters and they came and carried him in. You may remember, as you were there at the time."

I did remember M. being brought in suffering apparently from a bad go of malaria. I also remembered the doctor saying that there was more to it than malaria and that M. should be packed off to England on long leave. In fact, he never returned to Burma.

I turned again to Maung Yon, who was still there at my feet looking rather relieved to have got this off his chest and at the same time a little doubtful as to how it would be received. I thought I would test him for a change.

"Maung Yon" I said, "Can you account for the bell? Remember that others heard it besides yourself, even those who did not see or know of the incident."

"All I can say, *Thakin,* is that Nga Kywe was there and it was his bell that we heard."

"You mean that you believe that Nga Kywe was there in flesh and blood."

"Yes, *Thakin,* I and the others had no doubt on that score, for next morning we found his footprints. They had come up to a point about thirty yards from the hut, apparently waited there and then gone back the way they had come. What was more, they were the gait of an elephant being ridden, different as you know to that of a riderless animal."

"But" I countered, "how do you know it was Nga Kywe at all? It might have been one of the other elephants round about."

Maung Yon gave me what I can describe only as a look of pity. "Surely, *Thakin,* you know the *oozies* can tell each elephant by its prints! Apart from that, I should tell you that the prints were followed back by a party the next day and they came up with and recaptured Nga Kywe and no other! He had returned to near the place where the killing took place. The broken spear lay near by."

"What about the blood on the steps, Maung Yon" I asked, "was it there in the light of the day?"

"Yes, *Thakin,* it was."

"Do you expect me to believe that it was the blood of the corpse?"

"Believe it or not, *Thakin*. It is true that M. *Thakin* had cut himself on the broken tumbler, but that was not much. If you don't want to believe what I told you I saw, then doubtless you will say that it was his blood."

"You are sure" I said, "that the headman had nothing to do with the whole show? You've said that he was very angry and I know that he was a vindictive man."

It was a silly thing to say and I should have known better, but Maung Yon was quite equal to it.

"Thakin" he said quietly but deliberately, "I have only told you what I saw. If you think, you will realise that the headman could not have recaptured Nga Kywe and ridden that elephant himself by night to the hut; nor could he possibly have made himself look like that corpse looked; nor could he" and here a note of scorn crept into Maung Yon's voice, "have splashed blood all over the place, blood which you would like to believe came from a few small cuts on M. *Thakin's* hands."

"TAWTHA"

The author of The Discharge *wishes to remain anonymous. There is therefore nothing to be said about him except that he is an "old Burma hand" like the others and was an experienced jungle wallah, which is just what* Tawtha *means in Burmese.*

However, this can be said about his story. Giving a discharge to a deceased employee was an accepted custom in Burma, particularly in the rural areas. In cosmopolitan Rangoon it was not normal practise in the large European firms, but upcountry a posthumous discharge certificate would be expected.

Tawtha *leaves the reader otherwise to believe as much as he or she cares of his story.*

TEN

"THE CHICAGO OF THE EAST"

by Alan Prentice

In 1890, one of my predecessors as Agent of the Irrawaddy Flotilla Company in Bhamo was so optimistic about the trade through Burma into China that he made the prophecy, "Bhamo is bound to become in time the Chicago of the East."

It is not possible to write about Upper Burma when the British ruled there (1886-1948) without recalling the dreams of trade on the trail between Bhamo in the far north of Burma and Tengyueh in the Yunnan Province of China, a distance of only 130 miles. Nor is it possible to avoid frequent references to the part played by the Company I represented in Bhamo for a year in 1939/40; the Flotilla Company were very much part of it all and would of course have seen an immense increase in the river trade had these dreams been fulfilled. By the time the optimistic Bhamo Agent uttered his forecast of things to come, all the evidence we have points to any such hopes having been abandoned many years before. It all came about like this.

Missions to Burma by British diplomats from 1795 onwards endeavoured to establish relations with the Kings who reigned in Ava and Amarapoora, six hundred miles up the Irrawaddy River from the southern seaboard. These excursions had the objective of creating good relations and furthering trade, but little was achieved.

In the year 1836, ten years after the British annexation of part of Lower Burma, Captain Simon Hannay, an officer at the British Residency at Ava, then the Burmese capital, was allowed by the King of Burma to proceed north beyond Ava, but only because he was going into Assam to help the King resolve problems he had there with his Indian neighbours. Hannay got as far north as Bhamo and became the first observer to report on the existence of the mule caravan trade between Bhamo and Yunnan.

Kings of Burma kept a jealous eye on their northern territory, making it forbidden to prying eyes. After Hannay, the north remained closed to foreigners until in 1863 Dr. Clement Williams, at the time British Resident at the Burmese Court, by then at Mandalay, and a man much favoured by King Mindon, received permission to make his way into Yunnan via Bhamo. He succeeded in reaching Bhamo on a steamer lent by the King and was the first to declare that the Irrawaddy River was navigable by steamers to that point in the upper reaches. But delays followed and Dr. Williams was never allowed to proceed beyond Bhamo; he was forced to return to Mandalay with his knowledge of the trail confined to information he was able to glean from Chinese traders that he met in Bhamo.

By these accounts, and by evidence after the British did gain access to the trail, much trade was being carried over the route; salt and cotton to China as a basic and Chinese silks on the return journeys. Jade and amber were also exported from Burma, and, of course, contraband such as opium passed across the trail.

The glittering prize of a route into China then attracted French interest. In 1866/7 an expedition made a perilous 4,000 mile journey from Saigon up the Mekong River into Yunnan, but this only proved that a trading route would be unworkable. However, the very fact of French presence in Yunnan served to arouse greater British interest in the Bhamo route and pressure mounted for the prospects to be thoroughly explored. So Major Edward Sladen, then the British Resident in Mandalay, set off for Bhamo in 1868. King Mindon had relented and now wanted to encourage trade. The Suez Canal was soon to be opened; the sea route to Rangoon from Britain would become the shortest way to China and the dangers of the China Sea would be eliminated. Everything seemed to point to Bhamo becoming a very important place indeed.

Against almost unsurmountable odds, Sladen traversed the caravan trail from Bhamo to Tengyueh and returned to report favourably on the prospects for British trade. The following year a British Political Agent was sent to Bhamo, the Irrawaddy Flotilla opened a regular steamer service from Mandalay to Bhamo and Sladen pressed for the building of a railway from Bhamo to Tengyueh. Five years of vacillation followed before British and Chinese Governments both agreed to a survey to examine the railway proposal. But tragedy struck at the survey parties, the British leader of one being murdered and of another ambushed; the Chinese hill people did not want a railway. It all seemed too difficult and the Governments turned deaf ears to commercial appeals for action. Historians believe that if the French had continued their interest the British would undoubtedly have explored more seriously the proposal for a railway. So the mule caravans still walk the Bhamo / Tengyueh trail today.

Yet fifteen years after that last survey the Bhamo Agent who made the Chicago prophecy still believed that the trail would become a major route for trade between Britain, India and Burma on the one hand, and the masses of Western China on the other. The hopes seem to have died hard.

The euphoria had long since evaporated by the time I arrived in Bhamo in 1939. The trail was still carrying a certain amount of trade and the caravans were to be seen coming and going. By my time the trail terminated some 17 miles from the town of Bhamo at a village called Kyigondap; there a number of Chinese Inns or caravanserais formed the terminus where the animals were loaded and unloaded. There was a motor road from Bhamo to this point, but thereafter the trail deteriorated to little more than a slippery muddy path in the rains and traversible only on foot or horseback, a deterrent to all but the most venturesome.

It can best be described as a rough 'bridle path' fashioned by the trample of countless feet, human, animals of burden and horses, over the ages and worn by the erosion of water, leaving ugly outcrops of rock. Only four feet wide at places, it follows the valley of the Taping River for much of the route and continually crosses steep contours, sometimes to reach a village; some hill tribes seem to site their dwellings on mountain tops. The route rises to 5,400 feet at the Tengyueh plain and is mostly over Chinese territory, the frontier being only 51 miles from Bhamo.

The caravans I saw were composed mainly of mules, but bullocks were also used, always overladen with merchandise piled to astonishing heights. The unfortunate animals bore evidence of old scars and constantly suffered from sores plagued by flies; the rugged men who drove them showed little concern for their well-being. They were mainly Yunnanese in origin, all in some contraband racket, a law unto themselves. A caravan would consist of over a hundred animals and ferocious Chow dogs went with them for protection against robbers who roamed on the trail. Passengers, normally the owners of the goods being carried, were borne in hammock-like stretchers by two men, sometimes with an awning for cover from the elements.

At the Burma end of the trail, customs and police kept a close watch in search of contraband, which was only found when new places of concealment were exposed. A raid on to the trail itself was more often than not met by a warning to the caravan, when everything and everyone, men, animals, and dogs, would disappear into the countryside; in a matter of seconds the trail would be deserted.

Opium was the main item of contraband. The great poppy fields of China produced vast quantities of opium and there was a ready market in Burma for it, a curse yet a benefit to mankind at the same time, a good servant but a bad master. The Burmese Kings had strict rules about its use and under British rule in Burma cultivation of the poppy was illegal. This did not solve the problem of addicts, who had to have it to sustain life itself, and licensed opium shops were set up to provide for their needs. During the Japanese war the shortage was exploited — war is war — and as an Intelligence Officer in the Kachin Hills I used it as payment for information.

There was something of a revival of interest in the old trail and of trade into China when I was at Bhamo. The Japanese war with China was raging in 1939/40 and with China's eastern seaboard ports all closed the route through Burma into Yunnan became a vital means of supply for the hard pressed Chinese. A road of sorts from Bhamo existed and took traffic through to the main Lashio / Yunnan road, via Namkham; over it went supplies brought in to Rangoon by sea and up the Irrawaddy to Bhamo. The Tengyueh trail was of little value to this kind of traffic, and indeed would not have been trusted with it, but there were changes in the old pattern of trade which our nineteenth century adventurers had discovered there. Salt was urgently needed in China and was coming up from Lower Burma in our flats (barges) in complete 500 ton loads to be broken down into bags suitable for the mule panniers. Ginned cotton from central Burma, now tightly baled with iron bands, was broken down on the foreshore at Bhamo into pack size, the bands being eagerly purchased by Yunnanese blacksmiths who converted them there and then into swords. It was very much a one way traffic from Burma to China, for there was little silk to be had for export from Yunnan.

The ancient Chinese Joss House at Bhamo.

The most important event in what was for me an eventful year in Bhamo was the part I had to play in the transportation of an aircraft factory from our steamers across the frontier into China. Hard pressed by the Japanese in their eastern provinces, the Chinese Government decided to site this factory just inside their border some seventy miles from Bhamo at a village called Loiwing. The American Curtis Wright Corporation despatched the whole factory in parts to Rangoon, flats and steamers of the Flotilla Company received consignments as they arrived, taking them direct from the ocean ships, and delivering them at Bhamo a thousand miles up river. I had then to arrange to get the parts ashore, including some very heavy and bulky pieces, and organise loads to enable them to be taken by road over the mountain range that separates Burma and China. Lorries had then to negotiate the unsurfaced road to Loiwing; the narrowness and gradients of this road made it impossible for vehicles to pass for 50 miles of its journey and a one-way traffic had to be ordered and controlled. This was the old Bhamo / Lashio Road on which Namkham lies, quite unsuited to heavy traffic. I went to Loiwing frequently and often beyond, deeper into China, as I was also Agent for a large road transportation Company taking much needed supplies to Kunming through Yunnan. When the American erection team had built quarters for themselves at Loiwing I was comfortably accommodated, but frequently I had to spend the night in Chinese Temples by the roadside.

Before a single aircraft built at Loiwing even took to the air in combat, the Japanese had discovered the ploy and bombed the new factory to bits. The only piece of humour to be extracted from this sad tale is the odd behaviour of my successor at Bhamo who happened to be in the Loiwing area when the bombing took place. He fled to the jungle and instead of lying down he climbed a tree. Ken Gourlie was never afraid to tell this story against himself and to add that as a Chindit, after we went to war with the Japanese, he soon learned that down the way was the proper direction to go when bombs began to fall.

Bhamo was a small town; during my time the population was around the 8,000 mark, frequently increased by nomadic visitors from the surrounding mountain tracts. They came in search of trade and bought at the famous local market, the focal point for a large area and a meeting place for many races. The resident population was composed mainly of Chinese, a lesser number of Burmese and Indians and a few Shan and Sino-Burmese cross-breeds.

A great variety of clothing was worn by the nomadic traders. Although some mountain folk wore dark and sombre clothing, the Kachins and Shans, particularly the women, brought a great brightness of colour. They were often adorned by a fine array of shining silver buttons, bangles and beads, while the men sported silver handled swords which glinted in the sun, usually braided with scarlet cords. It was a spectacle that one could never forget.

There was in Bhamo an outstanding brick and stone building, the Chinese Joss House, the best of its kind in Burma. This Temple housed large grotesque images in its dark interior, creating a sinister atmosphere. Huge carved horses with outsized nostrils and bearded Chinese Warriors of ancient history were intermixed with images of the Spirits of Health and Water which purported to retrace the pages of Chinese history. The atmosphere inside the Temple was always smoky, joss sticks creating an overpowering aroma. There were strange side rooms in which older Chinese traders of the town would sit in the evening smoking opium and discussing the events of the day. I knew many of these gentlemen, they were our shippers. On one occasion I was invited to share their smoke; one puff of an opium pipe was sufficient to last me all my life. Unfortunately the Joss House was destroyed during the Japanese War.

We had tourists in Bhamo. But they came as individuals not in the great numbers of today's tourists. They were mainly Americans, perhaps half a dozen at a time, and most would have taken the train from Rangoon to Mandalay and have come up to Bhamo by steamer to see the fine scenery of the upper river and the sights of our little town. In a day they would view the colourful market; China Street, where the industrious residents from over the border plied their trades; the famous Joss House; and would be driven out to Kyigondap if there was any chance of seeing a caravan. When a tourist once asked an English speaking resident what the sights of Bhamo were and was told that for tourists these were what should be seen, there was added "for residents, the tourists".

Although Bhamo was primarily a trading centre, during the British time it was a Government administrative centre controlling an area of over 7,000 square miles. A battalion of the Burma Frontier Force was garrisoned in the town. The European population of about fifteen was augmented by a number of Roman Catholic missionaries and nuns who extended their influence over a vast tract of country to as far north as Fort Hertz.

There was a good football field in the town. One of my predecessors in Bhamo had organised a football team which he had called 'Bhamo Rangers'. Composed mainly of Irrawaddy Flotilla staff, one or two youthful traders of the town, and, at times a Steel Brothers member of staff who had played international football for Burma. Our main support came from Roman Catholic Fathers who often occupied the front row of the little stand in our support (but made no attempt to have the Club name changed to 'Celtic'). As I personally financed the side and provided the jerseys and shorts (none of the players wore boots) I was, of course, the Jock Stein of the football world with the dubious advantage of being able to select myself in the side without any questions being asked. It was customary for native spectators to carry umbrellas in the rainy season and on one occasion an excited spectator, sitting near the touchline, used his umbrella to upend a swift winger; this created a near riot.

I paid several visits to Namkham, another frontier bazaar seventy miles from Bhamo, where the famous Dr. Gordon Seagrave had built his American Baptist Mission Hospital which served a large area of the Kachin Hills and deep into China. The hospital itself was immaculate for all its jungle situation, built of stone collected from the nearby Shweli River, more like a castle than a hospital. Here Karen nurses worked with Dr. Seagrave. He had a specially high regard for them, sponsoring them to the point where he himself fell foul of the Burmese authorities after the Japanese war and latterly went to prison for his cause, as it was thought that he was anti-Burmese.

Among Seagrave's patients were Sawbwas of distant Chinese Shan territories, one of whom was a constant visitor and whom he ultimately cured from otherwise terminal opium poisoning. But the great triumph was his success treating goitres, the common ailment of the mountain areas and particularly of women. The Kachins were greatly attracted by his successes and some made long journeys to be treated at Namkham. Dr. Seagrave often photographed goitre patients on arrival and again on discharge from hospital, the second photograph showing the removed goitre balanced on top of the ex-patient's head. This psychology worked well with Kachins and encouraged other sufferers to come in and have the operation carried out.

I said good-bye to Bhamo to return to Scotland on leave in

1940 not realising that I would never be back. But I came close as a soldier in May 1942 when I led my retreating party of Burma Frontier Force troops to a crossing of the Irrawaddy at Kyauktongyi, ten miles from Katha and some seventy miles from Bhamo. We had been guarding the airport at Heho in the Southern Shan States when I was instructed to retire and make for India. This apparently simple order resulted in a march of thirty days, during which we crossed the Chindwin River as well as the Irrawaddy, climbed over mountain passes exceeding 5,000 feet, and covered some 800 miles. The joys of living in Burma were temporarily halted then and for some months of recovery in hospital thereafter.

A. S. PRENTICE

Alan Prentice was my partner in the research and writing of Irrawaddy Flotilla. *I had known him when we were boys at the High School of Glasgow and when he joined me in the Irrawaddy Flotilla Company in 1935 an acquaintance grew into a lifelong friendship.*

When Burma was in Japanese occupation Alan spent two years at Fort Hertz in the Kachin Hills, one of the few posts in Burma to remain in British hands throughout the war. He was on intelligence as an officer of the Burma Frontier Force, involved with Kachin levies in harassing Japanese sorties from Myitkyina. When the war was over he became the first post-war Agent of the Flotilla Company at Mandalay.

Alan sought new pastures after river transport in Burma was nationalised in 1948 and went to Tanganyika as Managing Director of the road transport subsidiary of the Colonial Development Corporation. But this lasted for only two years and he returned to U.K. to spend the remaining years of his working life with Stonegate Farmers, an egg marketing co-operative in Sussex and Kent. Now he is retired and lives in Alfriston in East Sussex.

ELEVEN

NUANCES OF LOYALTY

by Noel Stevenson

It was the Easter weekend of 1941. We were not yet at war with the Japanese, but their attack on China was progressing fiercely, and as a tiny spin-off from that cataclysm I had been on a mission of destruction. My target had been the fields of opium poppies in the Kokang, a wholly Chinese area in the northernmost corner of the Shan States of Burma. The Kokangese had taken advantage of the fact that all official attention was focussed on the notorious Burma Road, which passed through my charge into China, and along which every kind of vice had burgeoned like the water-hyacinth in the flood of supplies of all kinds pouring across the border.

The Kokang was ideally situated for the clandestine production of opium. A place of sharp mountain ridges and a myriad hidden glens, romantically remote from the beaten tracks of motor transport and isolated by the turbulent Salween river. Not expecting an official visit that busy year, the Kokangese had really spread themselves, and every little glade was ablaze with blossom. Rumour had eventually reached my headquarters and I had had my orders — go and destroy.

Despite the evil nature of their crop I could not help feeling sorry for the people. We had spent a fortnight making them cut down their expected small fortunes, and they would be hard put to eke out their slender food supplies until the next harvest. Opium was the only exportable product of the Kokang really worth the arduous journey to the Shan markets, where it could be exchanged for considerable quantities of rice and other necessities, and the villagers usually managed to get away with enough well-hidden production to ensure their food supplements for the year.

I had found it impossible to persuade the Kokang *Myosa,* the Chief of the sub-state, of the justice of the Government's case. I protested in vain that opium was a drug, a bane, a destroyer of men's minds and bodies. Why then, asked the *Myosa,* did the

Government permit its sale in licensed opium shops in every town in Burma? And if we felt we must supply it to addicts in the plains, why did we have to buy opium from India instead of from the Kokang, where they needed the money to buy food? Besides, he added for good measure, what about the wives in his village who were tired of child-bearing and were in the habit of putting their husbands on to opium as an alternative form of solace? The logic of his arguments had left me with a deep sense of guilt about my destructive passage, not lessened by the fact that not one village had tried to interfere with it.

All this was passing through my mind as I lay awake waiting for the first rays of sunlight to blazon the painted door of the *Myosa's* handsome *yamen,* which I could just see through the open flap of our tent. It was our last day in the Kokang, and he and I would have a somewhat embarrassing parting. On the one hand I had ruined his people's immediate economic prospects, and he would be held partly to blame for having failed to persuade me to change my mind. On the other hand his reception committee by the roadside the day before had blown an alphorn blast of welcome that might have felled the walls of Jericho, and my hired pony had turned a back somersault over me, tearing the muscles of my right shoulder and leaving me unable to write or use the shotgun on which we usually depended for our suppers. Both of us would feel some loss of face.

My wife, Miggie, was still asleep, with her soft breath keeping time to the jerking chant of a girl pounding grain somewhere in the village below. I had brought her with me, despite the risk of trouble, because she was unlikely ever again to have a chance to see the home life of a Chinese state, and had been most anxious to come. I hesitated to wake her, for neither of us was looking forward to the knee-cracking descent of four thousand feet into the gloomy gulch of the Salween at the Gujatu ferry, and the subsequent long climb up on to the ridges of the Kachin Hills on the other side. I was still feeling sorry for myself when our Kachin bearer dumped a kerosene tinful of hot water under the bathroom flap and brought our tea. Miggie sighed and sat up without enthusiasm. Somehow we both felt it was going to be a trying day.

Since my torn shoulder prevented me from shooting for the pot, and I wanted to look tidy before the *Myosa,* I put on a white shirt, a decision I was to regret before the day was out. We

Crossing the Salween at Gujatu.

breakfasted leisurely, and let most of our jingling cavalcade of mules go ahead with my escort of two sections of military police while I had a last chat with the elders. The presence of an escort was in itself unusal, as I rarely took one with me on my travels around the border. Their passage was always a little alarming to the villagers and made it more difficult to get on friendly terms with them. But this occasion had been special. There had always been the slight possibility of trouble, though when it did come it was from an entirely unexpected direction.

Half way down the long descent to the river we came upon our men and mules halted by the bridle path, facing uneasily some thirty-odd blue-clad Yunnanese soldiers on their way up the hill. I went along with my Chinese Interpreter to ask the soldiers what they thought they were doing marching armed to the teeth through our territory. They were a surly looking lot, so I told my Interpreter to inform the officer in charge that he was lucky that he had met me first, as if he had come unexpectedly upon the main body of my escort following me down he might have found himself in trouble. He was not to know that my entire force was already standing in front of him. We were outnumbered nearly three to one: my men had only their rifles, while his party carried two bren guns in addition to their rifles, and most of the men had four stick grenades apiece. The officer himself wore a long-range Mauser pistol in a wooden stock-cum-holster strapped to his belt.

Happily the bluff served its purpose. The officer bowed obsequiously, explaining that they had lost their way and would be pleased to go wherever I directed them. I explained that they should not have crossed the Salween at Gujatu, as the path along the Chinese border lay over a ferry some ten miles to the north. They would have to recross the river and make their way northwards along the ridge above it. We waited while they turned about and then followed them down, quietly congratulating ourselves on avoiding a possibly nasty border incident.

It was mid-morning before we reached the dark river. The rocky bank on to which the path debouched sloped very steeply down into the ice-cold and fast-running water. It seemed a most unlikely place for a ferry, but a little bunch of Kachin youths on the other bank shouted out at our appearance and prepared to come over on a small bamboo raft. Four of my men who had gone ahead to warn the raftsmen were standing waiting a hundred yards along the rocks on our side of the river at a point where another track wound up into the Kokang. The Chinese soldiers filing along the thick jungle above the bank began to push up this track past my men, so I called them to come back, and pointed to where their path lay, across the river.

They all started to shout to each other rather excitedly, and in order to calm them down I told Miggie and my escort to wait where they were while I went along with my Interpreter to have a word with the officer, who was in the middle of the strung-out column. It took us a minute or two to scramble along the rocks below his men and I had just reached a point some ten feet below him when he yelled out in Chinese — "Shoot! Shoot!", yanked out his pistol and took a shot at me. He must have been sadly out of practice, for the bullet only burned the skin between my body and my folded right arm, slightly wounding my Interpreter, who was standing behind me, in the thigh. In what seemed like slow motion I thought — "Lord! What an ass I've been. I can't get up these rocks with only one good arm. I can't scramble back under their noses to rejoin my men. If I stand here the blighter will fire another shot and may aim better next time. What a day to be wearing a white shirt!" I folded over as if mortally wounded, wriggled a moment and lay still, gambling hopefully that my escort would open fire and distract attention long enough for me to get away. The crackle of rifle fire that came from them was the sweetest sound I've ever heard. I rolled down the bank into the rushing water, grabbing a rock to stop myself being carried away before I could collect my thoughts.

Eight grenades burst among the rocks above me without effect. Then a Bren gun along the bank opened up and the ripping splash of bullets clouded my glasses and I couldn't see a thing. I shouted to the Kachins on the other bank to fire on the Bren gunner to give me a chance to slip downstream towards my escort. There were loud booms as two Kachin youngsters fired their flintlocks, another long rattle of bren fire, this time not at me, two more loud booms and then silence. The two boys had been calmly re-loading their flintlocks behind a large banyan tree while the Bren gunner had been spattering the other side with a magazine-ful of bullets, and had then popped out and hit both the gunner and his mate with their second rounds of miscellaneous ironmongery!

I let the current sweep me fifty yards downstream to where I had left my men, but all had vanished. I feared the Chinese might have abducted Miggie and called her name a dozen times. Silence. I hurried back along the way we had come to see if they had all taken cover, and found that my servants had hidden Miggie among the jungled rocks. They said my escort had gone into the jungle after the Chinese, and I realised that they would not want to answer my calls for fear of disclosing their positions to the men they were hunting.

In ten minutes they were back, having lost their quarry, and we were able to piece our stories together. As soon as they had seen me fall my men had opened fire. Miggie had wanted to run to me but our cook had wisely pulled her into the river and behind a rock. The ricochets were flying around them thick and fast, so he and my Kachins had rushed her back along the path into safer cover to await the outcome of the fracas. They had thought I was dead and were astounded to see me bob up unhurt. One of the four men who had gone ahead had been shot by the Chinese, but the others had beaten off their attackers. We had lost the dead man's rifle but had picked up two Chinese rifles and a number of grenades. Several of the Chinese, including two of the Bren gunners, had been seen to fall and be helped away by their companions, and they had used up a lot of their irreplaceable ammunition, especially for the Brens. We had not come off too badly, considering the odds and my carelessness.

The Kachins who had crossed over the river to meet us said that the Chinese had been boasting as they came through their villages that they were deserters on their way to join a notorious bandit leader over the border further south. It seemed likely that our chance meeting with them had saved the *Myosa* from being their first victim. Now the would-be bandits had trapped themselves in a deep valley. Messengers ran up the hill tracks to warn the Kokang villagers to call in all their gunmen and ambush the intruders at the head of the valley as we went through it. We were just about to start when a village policeman called across the river to say that over a hundred more Chinese soldiers, also believed to be deserters, were already on their way to join the others and were at the moment about twenty-five miles away. I decided to leave our erstwhile attackers to the care of the Kokang villagers, and get on to the ridge on the Kachin side of the river where we would be well above and better able to deal with this formidable new influx.

The Kachins at the ferry were delighted at the news and at

Noel Stevenson's wife Miggie with the Hpawngseng Chief and some of his men.

once volunteered to help to repel the intruders. The youngsters who had silenced the Bren gun bounded off up the hill track like mountain goats to spread the glad news that every man with a gun was to join me as soon as possible. The cheerful little Kachin Chief of Hpawngseng was quick to ask if it would be in order to bring *all* the guns, including some — and here I half-detected a slight hesitation — for which they had not yet had time to apply for licences. I should have known from his innocent look that there was a surprise in store for me, but there was no time to be lost, so I said "Of course! Bring the lot and I'll register them when we've got rid of the Chinese."

Dawn next morning found us all in ambush along a steep bank above the fork where a track led back into China off the path to Gujatu. The Kachins chose their own places. This was their land and they knew every nook and cranny. I kept my escort at the pivotal point where the two tracks diverged. For more than a quarter of a mile every yard of the advancing soldiers' route was covered at point-blank range. Fortunately it was a dry day, so even the men with flintlocks had their guns cocked as they squatted in the jungle, most of them with their drawn swords on the ground at their sides ready for the onset that would follow the first volley. Parties of some twenty guns stood at the ends of the ambush, ready to close it once the Chinese were in. From the path itself not a man could be seen, nor a sound heard. I thought to myself — "I'm glad I'm not the one to be walking into this little lot!"

Miggie was above us in the Kachin village with a pony and a village policeman ready to take her out of harm's way if things got rough. The Kachin women and children had their own well-tried drill. They would simply vanish into the jungle, to reappear when all was quiet again. As we waited I became increasingly aware that I had committed myself to a course which could well end in dire trouble for me whichever way events turned out. We would not know for certain until things were actually happening whether the men approaching us really were deserters. If they were not, and we attacked them, I would have a massive international incident on my hands. If they were, and we did not act quickly and decisively, we could have real trouble of another sort. In either case the Yunnanese authorities, anxious to save face and unwilling to admit that their men were deserting, might well claim that we had launched an unprovoked assault on innocent allied soldiery. I wasn't feeling too happy. I had taken every precaution I could think of to ensure that our visitors took the path back into China without fuss, but there was always the chance that some trigger-happy loon among my Kachins would start a slaughter of potential innocents. They had no great love for Chinese soldiery, and even less for Chinese bandits.

We had two hours to wait, and the atmosphere was pretty tense when at last we saw the long blue file of soldiers rounding the corner into the re-entrant where the ambush lay in wait. We noted anxiously that there were six Bren guns and a mortar section among them. Soon the whole column was in the trap and I stood up with my wounded Interpreter and had him call quietly to an officer near to us to say that they were to take the path back into China or they would find themselves in trouble as their whole column was covered.

Once again the Chinese started to shout excitedly among themselves and my escort, who had lost a comrade, fingered their triggers joyously. In desperation we played our last peace card, and I signalled for the pre-arranged shout from all the hidden men that would let the Chinese — always nervous of the Kachins — know the extent of their peril. The sheer volume of sound was electrifying. For a second or two it was touch and go whether the Chinese would start shooting out of sheer panic, but then the officer to whom we had been speaking bellowed an order, and they all began to file down the path that led back to the border, tracked by a rearguard of exultant Kachins. The crisis was over, and our pulses slowly returned to normal. We confirmed later that the men had been boasting of joining the bandit gang, but that would now be China's problem.

That afternoon the escort cremated their dead comrade and we prepared to set off again after his killers. Before we could do so a party of Kokang villagers arrived bearing our missing rifle and one prisoner trussed up like a pig on a pole. Full of the joy of victory, they reported that all the other deserters had either been killed or had fled across the border. I asked no questions about the would-be bandits' weapons. If the Kokangese had them in the thatch that was all to the good. My headquarters at Kutkai on the Burma Road was much too far away to give them any help in the kind of emergency that had just arisen, and anyway I felt it would be some small return for the ready and effective aid they had given despite my destructive passage through their villages.

It took me the whole of the next day to carry out my promise to register the guns that had answered the call of the fiery cross. The Kachins watched me at work with interest, marvelling at the luck of the *Nampan Du*. The tale of my escape, as witnessed by their companions on the opposite bank of the river, had already assumed legendary proportions, and as my friends they were happy about it. But there was no doubt about what had made their cup of happiness overflow. It was not until I saw the serried ranks of Kachin warriors assembling with their unlicensed guns that I recalled the innocent look on the face of the *Hpawngseng Du* when he questioned me about them at the river crossing. Before the ambush there were only 145 guns listed in my register. After it the magical number was 777! The joke was certainly on me. The civil powers were notoriously sensitive about the number of licensed arms in the hands of the hillmen, and I would have a lot of explaining to do when I got back to headquarters.

TWELVE

ONE LONG PICNIC

by Hamish Mackay

Fright, they say, drives everything clean out of one's mind; but fear, or could you call it living in a constant state of fright, seems to sharpen the senses and leaves indelible impressions.

Some little time ago my old General said to me, pointing to his gullet, "Do you know, in all that time I just could not get a mouthful down past there." We were remembering Burma early in 1942 when the Japanese were surging round us, irresistible, arrogant, contemptuous of our totally inadequate defences. The General certainly remembered vividly every little incident that happened in these desperate days. So did I — and so did my wife Misha.

I was serving with the Burma Rifles at the time, not very effectively; everything was chaos and confusion. Misha was in Maymyo with our daughter Janet, not yet aged two, and her Karen nannie. Maymyo was the military headquarters station in the hills some fifty miles from Mandalay and Misha had become a nurse there at the British General Hospital. It soon became a very busy place with sick and wounded pouring in from Moulmein, the Sittang, Rangoon and the battles for the Irrawaddy. She was not a trained nurse but had Red Cross first aid training and was welcomed as an auxiliary nurse when mobilisation was called in 1941.

When told that however great the urgency nurses in hospital do not run, she implicitly complied. Maymyo hospital was bombed several times and everybody who could scampered out to the slit trenches; but Misha stalked from her ward, quaking with terror but afraid to show it.

One patient specially put in her charge was a Sergeant Peperil of the Scottish Rifles who had contracted tetanus from severe abdominal wounds. Totally unable to articulate, even to utter, he lay, his back rigidly arched in agony. Misha watched over him, tirelessly anxious to ease him in any way she could, eager to observe the least hopeful sign day after day it seemed and night after night, until one day she heard a murmur. Leaning down gently over him she asked what she could bring for him. At last he uttered again, not words but mere sounds while she patiently listened; and then, after a struggle, it came out. He said, "G'way woman yer pesterin' me!" Her heart bounded and she *ran* to report the good news. Peperil recovered and did well and everyone rejoiced.

By early April 1942 the enemy were closing in on Mandalay. One column swarmed past Maymyo intent on reaching the railhead at Lashio beyond. It was high time that the hospital was moved, and as quickly as it could be done a train was assembled to evacuate it, hopefully through Mandalay and north to Myitkyina whence it might be possible to fly patients and staff out to India. Then the Indian engine driver fled and soldiers had to work the train down to Mandalay, where it was bombed. The occupants, staff and patients, immediately took shelter below the embankment until they were recalled by a very angry doctor who bellowed in a voice that could be heard even above the noise of the exploding bombs, "Do you all want to die of typhus?"

That night the train crossed the Irrawaddy River and the great Ava Bridge — the only bridge — was destroyed behind it. Not much doubt about it being the last train. But before they got to Myitkyina a new complication occurred. The airfield there, the only one in the whole area, was totally congested with crowds of refugees clamouring for seats. It was chaos and an edict went out that every fit person who could be spared from duty should walk out to India.

Walk out — very well, that was not impossible for a fit person, but one would require to be extremely fit. The distance from the Irrawaddy valley into Assam is 200 miles and there is no road. Footpaths do exist between villages, but villages, usually a few grass and bamboo huts, are sparse. The country is heavily afforested, natural jungle intersected by steep water courses, many of them dry at this season. And at the frontier it climbs to ridge after ridge of mountain rising to 8,500 feet. Inhabited? Yes, like some of the remote highlands of Scotland, but not with sheep; hoolock monkeys, peafowl, a roaming tiger and lots of lizards and snakes, but one might march for days without meeting people.

The maps showed much of the ground as unsurveyed; but Misha was fit and she could be spared, and moreover she was not alone. She had Janet with her and her nannie, who had flatly refused to desert her and whom she, in turn, was determined to stand by now far from her home, in strange and increasingly hostile territory. So she felt she ought to make the effort.

Two hundred miles — no doubt much of it clambering — say ten miles a day at most — twenty days; no roads, so no transport, so carry everything you need; carry everything you've got! And that was a mosquito net and some tins of powdered milk. It was all Misha had been able to carry from her house in Maymo; everything else, furniture, linen, clothes, silver, crockery, everything had to be abandoned. But with a mosquito net and tins of milk they were not ill-provided when they joined the party with whom they were to travel.

A section, about thirty Indian sapper-surveyors under their officer, who were also marching out to India. Could anything have been more conveniently arranged than an escort of map-makers and engineers? And the engineering skill of the escort was soon put to the test, for at Mansi they had to build a little flotilla of bamboo rafts to float them and their stores on a nearby stream. This occupied a day and it was 1st May before the party finally got launched on the first of four idyllic days drifting or splashing through the shallows of the sun-chequered rivulets, over sandbars and below a dense canopy of leaves till it joined the Uyu River near Maingkaing. Here country boats were found, but only for one more day of idleness.

It was an increasingly anxious time for the party because they were moving directly across the line of the Japanese advance. They were now approaching the Chindwin River which the Japanese would certainly use; they might be bumped into anywhere, at any moment. So that evening the boats were left behind and the party marched by night to Homalin on the Chindwin. They approached the village stealthily, but all was well.

On the morning of the 7th the party set out again, headed for the west and the hills. This was the start of many weary days. Toilsome climbs to distant ridges, knee-jolting descents into stifling valleys and then the long drag again to reach a crest they had seen so far away in front of them when they broke camp at dawn. And this, day after day.

Ma Nyein, the Karen nannie, marched barefooted, her slippers having been thrown overboard by baby, emulating her nannie's action when nannie threw away her now useless bunch

They stopped to bathe in some "secluded" dell.

of keys. It was Ma Nyein's turn to contribute now to the wellbeing, if not the survival, of the party. Plodding on tirelessly she pointed out the plants whose roots or leaves were edible. She showed how to prepare them and she it was who cajoled or commanded eggs or a handful of millets, sometimes even a poor little chicken, from the jungle hamlets they occasionally encountered. This was Naga country.

Nagas were, or had recently been, head hunters and were fascinated by the baby's wheaten white locks. Sometimes they carried her and would stroke her white hair while Nannie, a tiny person for all her lion's heart, glared at them with defiant eyes daring them to harm her. And the march to this extent was ordered by her that it had to comply with the baby's needs. Halts were regulated by her time for water to be boiled or food prepared and her night-net had to be suspended from a branch and carefully arranged before the mosquitoes came to life and got busy.

And so the march went on. Rarely they might stop and bathe in some secluded dell. Then, briefly refreshed, on again, the mind a blank and muscles automatic.

Then one day the heavy midday silence was shattered by a bugle call; a British outpost or a camp perhaps. Hearts bounded and feet were lifted and they stepped out smartly. But there was no post, no guard, no sentry, merely a cowherd, an old soldier who had been a bugler once upon a time and still remembered some of his old skill.

However, the next day, the 13th, the party did reach Ukrul which had been a post, though there was no help for them there. But from Ukrul the route grew easier, though there remained two long, searing foot marches before a motorable road was reached at last. The end was near; Imphal, the capital of Manipur, was not very far away — but would it be occupied by who? — that was the nagging fear. It was soon put to rest by the arrival of a British lorry which quickly lifted the now jubilant party into the town, a town ruined by bombing only a few days before — a sure sign that the enemy was following fast. On the outskirts of the town there was a camp put up for refugees by the Indian Tea Association; over the gateway a banner declared in large letters "The Blennerhassettes Welcome You". They did too. Here, after sixteen days of travel, rough, exhausting and hungry, but not too unhappy, travel, my family found hot baths and a meal and a bed and security and rest.

I, who was supposed to be part of the rearguard to the retreating army, had arrived in Imphal two days before my wife! We met next day, 16th May, and I drove with her and Janet and nannie to the railhead at Dimapur to see them off by train for India, where a month later I followed them.

In July I was sent for by Army H.Q. and told to return to Burma taking a mission into the Chin Hills. This took time to prepare and it was early September before I found myself retracing the long climb to Imphal with, as my travelling companion for the day, of all people, Misha's brother Willy Liston, an Edinburgh doctor now a Major of Territorial Artillery. We had met by chance that morning, I not even knowing he was in India.

Thinking to impress him I took him to a hilltop that evening and pointing to the east over the seemingly limitless landscape of jungle covered mountain ranges said to him that was the country his sister had marched across.

For some time he gazed at it silent and then said with real disappointment in his voice, "And she didn't bring any plants back with her — not even seeds?"

By profession Willy Liston was a gynaecologist; by occupation in war he was a gunner; at heart he was still a gardener!

Colonel J. N. MACKAY D.S.O.
late Prince of Wales's Own 4th Gurkha Rifles

It could be said that Hamish Mackay is a Gurkha, in all but birth. He served the Army from subaltern to Commandant of the 4th Gurkhas, leaving the Regiment and India after Independence in 1947. His wife Misha was with him in India and Burma for most of his service.

The title of his story about Misha obviously belies the content. It was anything but a picnic. In truth, Misha Mackay's exit from Burma in 1942 became something of a legend. Her arrival to the safety of Manipur two days after her husband astonished not a few, for Hamish had been in the rear-guard of that long retreat and had won the D.S.O.

*During the stirring advance of the XIVth Army through Burma in 1945 a famous battle was fought for Mandalay Hill. General Slim described it * as "the fiercest hand-to-hand fighting . . . as a Gurkha battalion stormed up the slopes . . . and the hill was completely in our hands." That battalion was of the 4th Gurkhas, commanded by Hamish Mackay. In that campaign he was again decorated, with a bar to his D.S.O.*

When the war and his Indian service were over Hamish and Misha retired to his Morayshire homeland. Interrupted by periods of working in America and in London, there they stayed until Misha's death in 1966. He now lives in Sussex with his son (Hugh Mackay is Overseas Director of Save the Children Fund) often making long journeys to the far corners of the globe to visit old comrades and friends. With four score year behind him he conquers impaired mobility with the aid of sticks and his indomitable spirit. A recent visit to India took him to the present day 4th Gurkha regimental centre at the invitation of the Indian Officers, to find with unconcealed pleasure that most of the old traditions of the regiment live on.

* *Defeat into Victory* by Field-Marshal Sir William Slim, Cassel 1956.

Part of the moat and wall ($1\frac{1}{4}$ miles long at each of its four sides) surrounding the palace at Mandalay, showing damage caused by fighting in 1945.

THIRTEEN

A WALK IN THE RAIN

by Ritchie Gardiner

In the early part of 1942 conditions in Burma were chaotic. The Japanese had invaded the Southern part of the country in December 1941 and by May 1942 they had covered about 1,000 miles to capture the most Northerly town of Myitkyina. Considering the terrain and the fact that our forces were doing their best to stop them this was a considerable feat of arms.

Myitkyina was the end of the railroad and also to a large degree of civilisation. The Japanese never penetrated much further though there was a dry weather road of sorts which continued North for about 160 miles, first to a Government village called Sumpra Boom, and then finally to the last outpost of Fort Hertz. This area is a valley of a kind surrounded on three sides by an unbroken chain of mountains anything from 8,000 up to at least 15,000 feet. On the other side of these lies China to the East, Tibet to the North, and India to the West. The country is very broken, heavily forested and entirely uninhabited apart from occasional small villages near the road.

The climate is dry and pleasant enough for the winter months but from May, when the rains break, till October it is quite different with a fall in the neighbourhood of 200 inches. The effect of this on the vegetation, the rivers, and on travel in these conditions, can be left to the imagination. It may give a better idea of what this means when I say that the comparable figure for most of the British Isles lies between 30 and 40 inches in a whole year.

The mountain chain is slightly dented in five or six places by so called passes which vary in height from about 8,000 feet to the highest which is a little over 14,000 feet. Four of them lead ultimately into India and of these the furthest South is the Chaukkan Pass, the one with which we are concerned. These passes had all been crossed at one time or another in this or the last century but — and this is the crucial point — never in the rainy season. Even the most intrepid explorer would have reckoned such a venture an unpleasant form of suicide.

I have said above that the rainfall in this Northern tip of Burma was in the neighbourhood of 200 inches but on the India side it was believed to be nearer 300. There were no roads or tracks of any sort although a map in my possession actually does indicate tracks as though they existed. Considering the conditions, it will be obvious that no track or path would last for more than a season or two. Rain and vegetation would see to that.

The conditions in Myitkyina during the first week in May 1942 were distinctly unpleasant. I had already seen a similar situation in Rangoon in March before the Japanese took the city but had managed to get away by sea to India by the skin of my teeth. I had however been unwise enough to fly back in April to Central Burma where the Government was still attempting to function but beginning to buckle on its skates. The Commissioner to whom I offered my service suggested that I should take over the post of Deputy Commissioner in Yenangyaung, which embraced the oilfields of the Burmah Oil Company. This normally carries with it the additional post of District Magistrate with the powers of life and death. As a jungle man who knew literally nothing of law I felt, or should have felt, highly complimented but had a nasty sneaking suspicion, and asked for half an hour to consider the matter. Hurriedly I made enquiries from some more knowledgeable people who confirmed my suspicions, for it transpired that the Japanese had captured the oilfields about two days before. The Commissioner was rather taken aback when I told him but I sometimes dream of my arrival in Yenangyaung and reporting to the Japanese Commander that I had come to take charge of the civil administration!

Anyhow I thought that I would be better in the Army and was at once commissioned along with two friends (only verbally for I don't think we ever had it in writing). We were ordered to build roads and airfields in Bhamo and Myitkyina districts. We did have about a month on this job but had achieved very little when Bhamo was captured and Myitkyina threatened. On the 6th of May we received orders at Myitkyina to make our own way to India as best we could. My two fellow officers elected to go by the Hukawng Valley which was the accepted route of escape. It was however a mass of troops and refugees, mostly Indian, and with my previous experience in Rangoon, I determined to go further North, where I hoped that there would be less pressure and competition.

Our course lay together however for the first few stages. We had a rather hairy journey in a small van we had picked up. It was a trip of about 100 miles on a dirt road, passable enough in dry weather but quite different after rain. In many places the road had been cut out of steep hillsides where a slide over the "khud" meant the end. Slide we did most of the time but it was astonishing how quickly one adjusted to this. However, our speed was seldom more than 5 or 6 miles per hour and often enough the passengers had to get out and push over a particularly bad patch.

My friends left me after about two thirds of the journey to strike West into the Hukawng Valley. It is sad to relate that one of them died there probably from sheer exhaustion as much as anything else. Conditions were terrible on that route and it was reckoned that about 5,000 people actually lost their lives there. I continued on to Sumpra Boom where I found a party composed mostly of Burma Levy officers, several of whom I already knew. They were discussing the forthcoming trek and which pass we should attempt into India. They had a W.T. set in communication with their headquarters in India and asked if porters from the India side could be sent up to meet us should we use the Chaukkan Pass route.

This is a point where some mystery enters the play. We did not know it, but Major-General Wood, the Administrator-General of Assam, had been advised that the route was impossible in the rains, which were just breaking, and forbad troops to attempt it. This meant that there was no idea of laying on a rescue mission from the India side as was done on the other routes. The local Frontier Service officer in Sumpra Boom, John Leyden, who knew the area better than anyone else, said the same. Next day however we discovered he had gone himself with a tea planter from Assam called Millar. This shook us but we finally decided that we had little choice. Just as we were about to set off we had a signal from India to say that porters would meet us on the pass. All we had to do therefore was to get there and it was with comparatively light hearts that we set off on the 13th of May.

There were other parties or individuals besides ours leaving on different dates and it was not uncommon for the composition of parties to change, sometimes one or two people going ahead to join other parties or others behind catching up. We ended up seven Europeans, including a Captain Fraser and Sergeant Pratt. John Fraser had been an Assistant in the rice department of Steel Bros. before the war. At the time we are talking of he was Station Staff Officer in Myitkyina but had left his exit from there a little too late, being captured by the Japs along with Pratt who was from the 7th Hussars, then a tank regiment. How the latter became separated from his unit I do not recollect but it must have been a long way from Myitkyina. They were both tied up by the Japs but during the night Fraser managed to loosen himself, then freed Pratt and they both escaped North to join us. It is outside the scope of our story, but Fraser was subsequently attached to Wingate on both his expeditions into Burma and was awarded the Military Cross.

We were a pretty motley group. Apart from Fraser and Pratt, there was Ronald Jardine who was Lever Bros. representative in Burma and rather older than most of us. There were Bill Howe and Eric McCrindle, both officers in the Burma Levies. Sadly, the latter survived this walk only to be dropped behind the lines by parachute a year later when he was killed. We also had our signaller Corporal Sawyer, a Londoner, who was not at home in jungle. However, when his wireless was dumped he proved himself useful at cooking. Last but not least there was Noel Boyt, another Steels man but then a Burma Levy officer and generally accepted as the leader of our group. There were also three others, an Anglo Burman, a Shan and an Indian who somehow became attached to the party. Including Indian and Gurkha troops there must have been altogether about 200 people who set out on the journey, generally in small groups.

We managed to hire some local Kachins to carry food, principally rice, and it took us 13 days to reach the Pass. This "work in" gave us an indication of what lay ahead but only that, for we had the Kachins and were not unduly laden. The first six days were on a fair dirt road, sometimes we were dry, sometimes we were wet, but always had a roof over our heads at night so there was no great hardship. However none of us were in the pink of condition. All had already passed through months of arduous retreat conditions, short of food and short of sleep, but seldom short of the need to make an extra effort, however tired.

A crisis occurred on the 20th May when we were due to leave the road and strike westward into the uninhabited foothills. The porters refused to budge unless we provided opium for the slog uphill. We had already agreed to pay them about three times the normal rate in silver rupees and had no opium. By a stroke of luck and some slightly underhand work on the part of one of our members opium was duly produced and all was well again. In this part of the world all really heavy work seems to call for such a "stimulant". It is chewed like tobacco and I personally tried a ration but with no appreciable effect.

By this time the rains had really broken and we were nearly always wet through. We were also beginning to realise that to be personally wet was of comparatively little importance. What did matter was to keep our rice from getting wet. We dumped our W.T. set and started off uphill, some very heavy going through deep mud. This was the first time we had to build a camp and were more than thankful that we had brought two tarpaulins for the roof. We also met here our first experience of leeches and polaungs. We were to meet them daily and all day for a long time to come.

A polaung is a small black fly (much smaller than a house fly), whose bite raises a blood blister which itches. Two or three mean very little but with bare knees — some of us had only shorts — and bare arms we were a real tasty morsel which they certainly made the most of. We were literally covered with bites and the swollen legs from which some of us suffered could well have been attributed to them.

A leech starts off no bigger than a match. If left undisturbed however it will suck enough blood to distend at least to the size of your small finger. If it feels satisfied at that it will drop off. One could not spend half an hour in some parts without having to remove up to 50 of these little suckers. They did not confine themselves to legs and arms. At one time or another we found them on or in every part of our bodies including even the mouth and other tender parts. Each may only have taken a small quantity of blood but some bites bled quite badly and we had not enough salt to prevent bites or to remove them gently. The cumulative effect of hundreds of bites meant a distinct loss of blood which we were not — at least in the latter stages of our journey — able to replace due to our starvation diet.

By the 22nd May we were rising into the hills and the temperature was dropping to the point where being wet and cold was a real hardship. I had nothing but web equipment for such spare clothes as I carried and found to my dismay that it was far from waterproof. It need hardly be said that our personal gear was not only of the scantiest but consisted almost entirely of what we had been able to pick up in Myitkyina. The term "pick up" would in peacetime be termed theft, but at least it was nearly all already abandoned by the previous owners.

On the 23rd our route lay entirely up a rocky stream. We were told we had 57 crossings to make but gave up counting about half way. Some had felled trees on which to balance precariously but mostly it was just a case of wading on slippery rocks against a strong current. The following day we were into pine country at an altitude of about 6,000 feet. We met here another party who were held up with a bad case of malaria. This was something to which we were all liable from our previous journeyings but our party were lucky to escape it. I personally was talking quinine as a prophylactic and it was very effective until the very last stages of our walk.

Our final day up to the Pass was dry and sunny but involved another trip of several miles up a fast and strong mountain torrent of ice cold water. Here the Kachins left us without wasting any time and nothing would induce them to accompany us any further. They said that if the rains really broke — we felt they already had — they would have great trouble getting back home. The Pass itself was a weird place, not at all obvious as a Pass, although the hills on either side run up to over 12,000 feet. This was largely because it was heavily afforested by trees which were gnarled and looked very old. They were mostly festooned with moss which gave them an unearthly and depressing appearance. There were quite a number of rhododendron trees anything from 30/50 feet high and the undergrowth was composed of ferns and bracken.

We felled some trees to permit signalling by smoke and flew a white sheet attached to a tall tree. From the 26th to the 29th May we waited anxiously for the help promised from India. We realised very clearly that if they failed us we would be dangerously short of foodstuffs, as we had only brought what we considered enough to see us to the Pass. There was some discussion as to whether or not we were actually on the Pass. There was also a possibility that the India party had missed us and were camped nearby — only too easy in this country. On the 30th we decided we had to make a move down to the river — the Diyun — which rose below us on the India side and which we proposed to follow. We hoped to meet the rescue party or at least to find traces of their passage if they had missed us.

This was where the real test began. There were no Kachins to carry the food, chiefly rice with a few tins of meat and some packets of biscuits. We divided it into roughly equal loads and reckoned that on half rations it might last us about 15 days. For spare clothes we had a couple of shirts and socks but very little else. The tarpaulins had to be left but most of us had a ground-sheet. I reckoned that my load including weapons was a little over 50lbs., nothing extraordinary for a young man on a day's march but now it was rather different. We got an early taste of this down a steep and rocky tributary of the Diyun where I fell three times, the last one off a boulder on to my face in the water. The river here was about 15 yards wide and we reckoned we would have to stick to one bank as it was uncrossable in most places. We seldom covered more than four or five miles in a day which generally began about 7 a.m. and ended about 3 p.m. We had to have time at the end of the day to build some form of shelter roofed as a rule with ferns or leaves, neither of which can be described as rainproof.

We were passed in the first days of June by a number of Indian and Gurkha troops while camped, and next day discovered to our dismay that we had "lost" some packets of biscuits and cheese. As against that I had the good luck to hear a barking deer, a small animal similar to a roe deer, and managed to shoot it crossing the river. This gave us our first real meal of meat since leaving Sumpra Boom and we had enough left to carry for two days more.

Perhaps I can best give an idea of the conditions by quoting what was quite a common type of day from my diary of 5th June.

"Ridge Camp to Diyun IV (Rising River Camp). 3 miles — 3,900 feet. After a miserable wet night due to a leaky roof, we did not consider it worthwhile attempting to light a fire and had an early breakfast of a couple of biscuits and a small piece of cheese. Got off at 7.30 a.m. on what promised to be our easiest march but we came down the ridge to find the Diyun rising and were unable to follow the track which seemed to lie along the base of a precipice and was submerged. The only course open was to cut a new route over the back of the precipice and as we were considering the matter the rain started again in real earnest. We decided to erect camp but very unwisely did so on a stone bank — part of the river bed — which was soon threatened by the rising water and we had to start all over again in a heavy downpour which chilled us to the marrow. We are still 3,900 feet up and to be soaked and cold is one form of torture. The leeches were particularly bad and I must have picked off 100 at least during the day. We can't really grumble of course for I've been expecting this kind of weather for about the last three weeks and we were very fortunate to get such a comparatively fine spell at the higher altitudes."

By this time we had given up hope of meeting the party from India and had begun to realise that their promise to meet us must have been based on a very optimistic view of the conditions they were likely to meet. As a jungle man I was always hoping for rafting water in the Diyun. It would have been so easy to cut bamboos and make a raft to float leisurely and without effort over many more miles that we could possibly have covered on foot in a day. There were occasional stretches of a mile or two where this would have been feasible but always at the end there would be a fierce rapid and boulders which would almost certainly have spelt disaster. However, any temptation to this course was ruled out because there were no suitable bamboos.

By the eighth of June our condition was showing signs of deterioration. Several of us had sores and swollen legs and feet which somewhat resembled beri-beri. This is a disease caused by a lack of vitamin B1, which debilitates and can ultimately cause death. Its principal outward symptom is a massive swelling of the limbs. If you pressed the swelling with your finger the depression which was made only responded very slowly. The party was also slowing up with the need for frequent rests. Signs of game were found but no game which undoubtedly had been disturbed by the parties ahead. We also found our first, but not our last, corpse.

On the eleventh we arrived at a big tributary of the Diyun which had to be crossed but was in flood and impassable. We were caught up here by another group and next day while we were searching up and down the stream for a crossing place they managed to get over. It was four o'clock in the afternoon when we decided to follow. Most of us made it without undue difficulty but Fraser fell in and was washed against a rock where his legs became wedged by a log although his head was just above water. Corporal Sawyer was standing by but was unable to help so I left my kit on a boulder in midstream and waded back. It would be about waist deep and a strong current. Sawyer, who was by this time in a badly weakened condition attempted the remainder of the crossing but fell in and was swept away. In spite of a search we never found him again. After a prolonged struggle and finally cutting off his pack, I managed to release Fraser's legs and we both staggered back to the bank from where we had started. After a much needed rest I returned to the rock in midstream and recovered my kit to complete the crossing, leaving Fraser to join another party camped nearby. Next day the river was down about a foot which made all the difference and we got him over fairly easily. We had however lost his pack and also Sawyer's. A recount of the rations showed we might have food for seven days allowing daily 4 ozs. of rice — by now definitely mouldy — one biscuit also very mouldy, a weak cup of marmite and about $\frac{1}{2}$ oz. of cheese.

On the 13th June we had for a change a dry and sunny day and were enabled to dry our clothes for the first time I could remember. The next day we managed to shoot a python after a fusilade of misfires from a revolver. It was a most disturbing experience to find that brass cartridges were damp and useless in spite of all we could do to keep them dry. Unfortunately the snake only gave us a mug of soup and a rather tough cutlet apiece. We had some fish hooks and I baited a couple with python liver but had the usual fisherman's luck.

By this time the deterioration in our condition was becoming quite marked. All were weakening and inclined to be irritable. Speech itself was an effort and so indeed was thought. We were not cheered either by finding corpses or people who were left behind too weak to proceed on their own. Most of us were also beginning to sleep very badly even though exhausted. We generally started off each day in a spirit of optimism, expecting round each corner to come at least to the beginning of the end, but as each corner failed us we became more tired and dispirited. On 18th June we made a recount of the rations to find about 5 lbs. of very mouldy rice and 9 packets of biscuits in an even worse condition, with a bottle of marmite and a tin of cheese thrown in. This to do ten people as we now were. We reckoned it might do us four days but were well aware that it was, or would have been if in good condition, about one tenth of a normal ration.

Our luck however was to change at long long last!

June the 19th is a day which stands out in my memory. It was the 37th day of our struggle and we expected quite a few more before reaching a village where we might hope to find succour. We started off with an abortive attempt to use a small raft which we found and after coming across two more corpses, we suddenly came face to face with some Mishmi tribesmen. They actually turned out to be looking for us. We could hardly believe it but they had a note from one of our friends who had gone ahead and also one with the signature "Gyles Mackrell". The latter said he had heard there were some Europeans attempting the long walk and was accordingly sending them — the Mishmis — up on spec. They said that his camp was about two days march away. Knowing that help was at hand we had a "feast" that night and topped it off with a smoke of some very black tobacco which they produced. Next day we made nearly 5 miles in a march of mental bliss but physical agony. My feet by this time were raw and inflamed all over including a large part of the soles and my boots, which were canvas, literally on the point of falling off. This day we met a party of Gurkhas from the Assam Rifles carrying stores to support the advance party of Mishmis who were continuing up the river.

On the 21st we were told we had only about seven miles to go but shortly after the start Sergeant Pratt, who was in a very weakened condition, said he could not go on. Fraser and I opted to stay with him while the rest went on. Next day we were met on the way by Wilson, a teaplanter from Assam, with some porters and, luxury of luxuries, I was able to hand over my pack and weapons and hobble cheerfully along with nothing to carry. By eleven o'clock we had reached the Dapha River. This was the Diyun's biggest tributary, the crossing of which we had feared from the start. Elephants then appeared from the other bank and we mounted them to ride across. The Dapha here was perhaps 70-80 yards wide and about 5-6 feet in depth with a very strong current. We could never have made it without their assistance and even the elephants found it far from easy. Indeed I had an uncomfortable few minutes wondering if I was going to follow Sawyer literally within fifty yards of our goal.

From then on we had ample food though we did not always think so. Mackrell, who was camped there, told me that he had to limit our input. Quite a number of the Indian troops who had arrived before us had been very ill for several days through eating more than their empty stomachs could cope with. I experienced this myself to some degree and realised the wisdom of his rule. We remained at the Dapha camp resting and

Elephants crossing the Dapha River in torrent.

Arrival in India. The party which walked, Ritchie Gardiner standing third from right.

recovering some strength until the 1st of July. We still had a week's journey to reach civilisation but it was with elephants and porters and *food,* so I shall end the account of our journey here.

In retrospect I think it safe to say that our rescue was entirely due to Gyles Mackrell. He had been some days away on another job when Leyden and Millar happened to contact him. Leyden being a Government official had been able to "induce" porters into accompanying them. They had therefore more food and were able to travel much quicker than us. They told Mackrell that other parties were almost certainly following them. Mackrell knew of General Wood's veto on attempts to use this route. He was however a civilian and a very senior planter and realised that rescue efforts must be made at once. With the support of the local chief he collected elephants and porters and force marched to the mouth of the Dapha, arriving to find the first of the Indian troops marooned on an island near the far bank. About 70 in number they apparently had been without food for some days. After several abortive attempts the elephants got them across and a couple of hours later the island was swept away by a raging torrent of snow water.

This was a point which none of us had hitherto appreciated, namely that the Dapha rose on the slopes of a mountain about 16 miles away. It was over 15,000 feet high and had snowfields which even at that season ran down to nearly 10,000 feet. Apart therefore from the rain there was a daily melt of snow which started at sunrise. If the melt coincided with the rain, as it so frequently did, the resulting torrent was frightening to watch and was accompanied by a roar that made speech difficult. This was largely caused by the boulders on the river bed actually being carried down *en masse.* We witnessed this more than once during our stay. At this season the only hope that a man might have had would have been in the early morning after a dry night, with perhaps a length of bamboo to help keep him afloat. Leyden and Millar had managed the crossing only by a lucky stroke of timing and weather and by forming a chain with their porters. This meant that if one man lost his footing the others were able to hold him, but there was a real risk of the whole lot being swept away.

It was hard for us to believe, but we were told we had had a comparatively dry spell; any one of the twenty or so tributaries which we had crossed could have held us up for two or three days. As I have said before, our rescue (and that of the others) was due entirely to the quick passage of Leyden and Millar and their fortuitous and very lucky contact with Mackrell. We had silver, we even had gold and we had opium, but they were of no value whatever and our brass cartridges were latterly quite unreliable had we met any game.

In a way the journey was an excellent illustration of what the human body can survive; hunger, cold, wet and leeches, not to mention cuts and sores. These healed cleanly at first but latterly tended to go septic. Foot sores were bad enough but in some cases hand sores developed which were another serious hindrance as we all had to carry a staff for wading and climbing. We did however have a stroke of luck for someone had "picked up" a supply of M&B 693 before leaving Sumpra Boom and we found this of great value. It is one of the sulpha group of drugs. I had never even heard of it but there is little doubt that it helped to keep us on our feet and in one case at least served to check an incipient bout of pneumonia. My own normal weight is about $10\frac{1}{2}$ to 11 stones but on arrival at the Dapha camp the Indian doctor, whom Mackrell had brought with him, said I was about 8 stones. I certainly looked it.

There were others behind us who were ultimately kept alive by air drops of food and finally rescued by a herculean effort which entailed the manhandling of boats up the Diyun, all organised and directed by Mackrell.

There could only be an estimate of those who attempted that journey and only an estimate of those who died but the number to have lost their lives was known to be at least twenty and may have been much higher. What would that number have been without the ability and the determined action of Gyles Mackrell? He was awarded the George Medal for the part he had played in the rescue.

FOURTEEN

DENIED THE ORDINARY RITES

by Hamish Mackay

Some time after the war with Japan a memorial was unveiled near Rangoon dedicated to "27,000 men of the Commonwealth forces who died in Assam and Burma in the defence of freedom to whom the fortunes of war denied the ordinary rites accorded to their comrades in death". Their names are inscribed on the memorial. Among them may be found that of John Henry Mackay.

John Mackay was a District Forest Officer in Burma when the Japanese invaded that country in 1941. With many others whose jobs had packed up he walked into India and sought employment there — if possible as a soldier. He was seen by the officer in charge of the Burma Surveys and on his recommendation was commissioned to the Indian Engineers and appointed to the map section at Imphal. His wide acquaintance with Burma made him valuable to the department but it was more than the face of the country that he knew — his knowledge of the forests and of the people and their language was profound and he longed to be used in a more intimate and more active role.

An organisation known as Z Force, consisting of men from the Burma services who were willing to return there, had come into being and was growing up. Two of its members, Webster and Castens (also forest men) carried out a mission into enemy occupied Burma at the turn of the year 1942-43. When they got back to India they went to Mussoorie and there met John Mackay on leave from Imphal. Webster, who wrote a report on what followed, here takes up the tale.

"The Z organisation was, at that time, frightfully secret and we who belonged to it used to pass ourselves off as Commandos, or Movement Control or what have you. But in John Mackay we found a very likely recruit and as the organisation was to be expanded (largely because of the success of our first mission) we came to tell him quite a lot about the racket. As soon as he knew what it was about John volunteered to come in.

We had a lot of trouble getting him out of the Survey people. Colonel Shelley, our number one, had to go to the top men in the department. Their objection to letting John go was that his eyesight was peculiarly suited to stereoscopic work and they wanted to reserve him for the interpretation of aerial photographs of the forests; they regarded him as one of their key men. Our retort to this was that another forest officer with stereoscopic vision could surely be found and posted to the Survey, whereas for Z Force, a man not only required unusual qualifications but he also had to be a volunteer. Even then John's people continued to be sticky and it was not until we reached Imphal on our way into Burma again in September, 1943 that we were able to prise him loose from his unit to join us.

The charter for our new mission, as for the last, was that we were to get behind the Japs and stay there until either the break of the rains (May the following year) or until our own troops caught up with us, whichever happened sooner — but if things got too hot for us we had permission to clear out. I should explain here that the Z racket was "Intelligence behind the enemy's lines" and that our job was to keep tabs on the Japanese, each in our own allotted area and to send out all the information we could by wireless. John had not been in on the planning discussions, but in any case Bertie Castens and I had decided that we would go in as a combined party and break off to our respective areas later, by which time John would be well in the picture.

During October we made our way down to the Chindwin to feel out the situation. At that time the right bank of the Chindwin was British territory, the left bank Japanese. While we were engaged in this manner, a Colonel Towers of the Royal Engineers, who was also on a Z job, appeared on the scene.His task was to make a quick dash to the Jap airfield at Indaw — and out again. After some discussion he decided it would be better to go in with us than to take a chance on his own.

And so at midnight on 31st October, under the very noses of the Nips, it was as one party that we slipped across the Chindwin and into the jungle beyond.

Men on a Z patrol had to carry all their gear and belongings on their backs. In addition to our weapons we carried our wireless sets and rations for seven days. On top of this, our ordinary load, we were carrying spare wireless sets. The reason was that on this expedition we were to be supplied by air and none of us could take the risk of his set failing nor the risk of having a replacement set dropped from a plane; our wireless sets were lifelines.

The first dropping zone (D.Z.) had been arranged at the point we expected to reach on the seventh day's march. We only just managed to make this rendezvous and duly received a drop there that night. We restocked our packs, buried what we could not carry and set off to our next D.Z. where we received another drop four days later. Here we made our second dump.

It had not all been plain sailing. Perhaps through sleeping in sodden clothes after a night march John had caught a chill. We were now well behind the Japs and had at all times to remain packed and ready to be up and off at a moment's notice. I say 'behind' but 'in the midst' would more correctly describe the situation; we were very close to them. We had in fact arrived at the point where we parted company. Bertie and John went one way and Zaw Gawng* and I another. Thereafter we laid on supply drops separately as we required them.

I came again to the second dump about 12th December to meet Towers who expected to have accomplished his mission, or to have done as much of it as he could, and to be on his way back to Imphal. He had no wireless set of his own and so I had to arrange a rendezvous for him on the Chindwin with V Force who were to help him across.

Towers told me when we met that he had left Bertie and John three or four days earlier. He said that while he was with them a call had been received from headquarters asking for an urgent report on an area farther north. John was ill at the time so it was arranged that he should remain in their present locality with three Kachins* while Bertie went north with the remainder. John was lying up in the Nam Kehu valley three or four miles from the only village in the neighbourhood. This village, a Naga village, had been visited and appeared to be trustworthy.

Towards the end of December I received information that a company of Japs had gone up to the Nam Kehu valley to search

* Webster does not mention where and when Zaw Gawng and the other Kachins joined the party, but it can be assumed that this would be at Imphal. Zaw Gang was a Burma Rifles Kachin officer, one was a regular Havildar (sergeant), the remainder levies.

for a British patrol. The valley is an elevated one enclosing the headwaters of a stream that bears the same name. It is very wild and rugged and is densely forested and is approached by only a very few paths. Ordinarily it would make an ideal hide-out but now it appeared that the enemy's attention had been directed to it.

I at once sent a message to headquarters asking that Bertie and John be warned that the Japs were on their trail. I could not communicate with them direct because our codes, for reasons of security, were different and we could therefore only pass messages to each other through Force headquarters.

Some time after this I had a disquieting message that read "Bertie O.K. Mac missing. Have you any news?" The expression 'missing' was applied to an officer or party if no communication had been received for a week. I decided I must go and find out what had happened. Accordingly I moved off east and arrived at our second dump on or about 10 January 1944. I stalked the dump with great care as there was every likelihood that I should find a Jap piquet waiting for me there. I found instead the three Kachins, Havildar Hpawpawng Naw and two others, who had been left with John.

From Hpawpawng Naw's story and from information gathered from other sources since it appears that John, though far from well was, early on, himself able to pay a visit to the Naga village. Afterwards Hpawpawng Naw visited it two or three times to get news. Everything seemed all right but on the last occasion he grew suspicious when the villagers invited him to enter the village and partake of a meal. He thought this was a trap and declined to go.

The villagers did not know exactly where the party was in hiding; all they knew was that it was somewhere nearby and this the headman must have made known to the Japanese at Kyaungale, their H.Q. thirty miles away in the plains.

The Japs turned out a battalion, posted piquets on all paths leading out of the valley and together with 500 villagers brought in from the plains proceeded to comb the area. It seems that the search went on for some days.

About the 18th December Hpawpawng Naw went to his party's latest dump and dug up some rations. As he turned to go he bumped into a heavily camouflaged Japanese patrol. The Japs, though they were out looking for trouble, were evidently as greatly startled as Hpawpawng Naw, for they bolted.

Hpawpawng Naw thereupon picked up the rations he had dropped in his excitment and returned to John's hide-out, less than half a mile away.

John was quite ill by this time — like all forest men he was subject to severe attacks of malaria and probably now suffered from a bout brought on by the chill. Nevertheless he was able to take in the situation and agreed that the party should pack up immediately and move to new quarters. His three Kachins supported him but after a mile and a half he was forced to call a halt. Next day they made as much again but by then John had reached his limit and could do no more. His men built him a shelter in the jungle near the head of a waterfall and there the party stayed. On the 22nd a number of Japanese and Burmans came up the stream to the foot of the waterfall but they turned there and went the way they had come. John was delirious at the time and was muttering and calling out but the noise of the falling water drowned the sounds. On the 24th December he died.

His Kachins laid him out in accordance with their own animist rites with his possessions, watch, sten gun, mess tin and so on laid beside him. They brought away his notebook and wallet containing his code and some photographs. Then they went up to a ridge along which they expected Bertie to return and they lay there for three or four days in order to warn him.

But there was no sign of Bertie, so Hpawpawng Naw returned to the dump where he had run into the Jap patrol and having collected more rations there he set out with his men for the second dump — which was generally recognised as a meeting place. As they went they paid a visit to John's shelter and were surprised and mystified to find that although it was the eighth day after his death, the body remained unchanged. No decomposition had set in (as it does very quickly in Burma) and they knew that the nats had taken him under their protection.

The journey to the second dump was quite a feat. The Japs were still searching the valley; Hpawpawng Naw had no map; many of the outward marches to the Nam Kehu had been made through pathless forest and sometimes by night; but Kachins have a sense of their own in the jungle and are never at a loss.

It was the havildar's intention to wait at the second dump for ten days in the expectation that I would turn up there. Actually I reached the dump on the third day after his arrival, but had I failed to put in an appearance he had planned to return to the

Nam Kehu to wait there for Bertie. He wished to take me back with him to the shelter in the valley where he was convinced we should find John's body still in a state of preservation, but this was not possible at the time.

In the second week of February I had another alarming message, this time about Bertie who was reported to have been last on the air on January 28th. Again I went east and again stalked the second dump and found Bertie there. Things had got too hot for him up north and he had been forced to abandon his wireless set. He had then sought out his spare set which had been left hidden by the Nam Kehu,but when he tried to use it it broke down. This was the call heard at headquarters on the 28th January. He did not know of course what had happened to John.

Bertie and I then took stock of our own position. We were much relieved to have met but we felt none too happy. The Japs were swarming round us and were looking for us. Our supplies were running low but we dared not take another drop because by this time the enemy knew exactly the implication of Dakotas circling overhead at night. There was no sign as yet of the anxiously awaited British advance.

But all this was suddenly changed early in March when, without warning, Wingate's airborne expedition flew in to strike the first electrifying blow for the liberation of Burma."

Webster's and Castens' excitement can be imagined as they watched the great aerial armada pass overhead. Unknown to them, this had largely been planned on the information sent back by their patrols. Eagerly they hurried to where glider after glider cast loose in the sky and circled to land; and in course of time they were flown out to Imphal.

For their outstanding services Webster, Castens and Zaw Gawng were decorated and there can be few who earned distinction more devotedly than they. John Mackay's name was also sent forward by his commanding officer, Colonel Shelley, who hoped that he too might receive the Military Cross, but it is an award that is not made posthumously; instead he was mentioned in despatches. Havildar Hpawpawng Naw was awarded a well deserved Burma Gallantry Medal while the levies, his two companions, were recommended to the Government for civil awards.

Wherever they have had the slightest evidence to guide them the Imperial War Graves Commission have been at enormous pains to recover and bury the bodies of our men. Happily John has eluded them. Even his comrades, the three Kachins who alone know his resting place, must have dropped back into obscurity for they were, as they said of themselves, *'lu nge'* — little men. The expression was used by Hpawpawng Naw when taxed with the question why he had not buried their dead leader. He replied, "We are little people and might be thought to have done him harm, so we left him where he could be seen."

* * * * *

I met Zaw Gawng, then a Captain in Z Force, in 1945. My battalion had just crossed the Irrawaddy at Thabeitkyin and he came to ask permission to pass through our outposts into the hinterland beyond, held by the Japanese. I did not know him, but I was not concerned about the risk to security; his credentials were good and in any case we had now a firm hold on the east bank. Yet I demurred; the ground he wished to cross was ground that my Gurkha patrols entered with caution.But Zaw Gawng made light of it.

He had of course been given my name when he was sent up to me and in the course of explaining his work he learnt that I was John's brother and straightaway went on to tell me substantially Webster's story which I have recounted here. I had not heard it before and it was all tremendously exciting. We had maps out and he showed me the Nam Kehu valley; but as he knelt with hand poised while he searched the contoured and tree-dotted green for the name, I knew where his finger would alight, for I knew the place; I had seen it!

It happened on a wonderful morning two months earlier, in December 1944, after a forced march in pursuit of the Japanese between the Chindwin and the Irrawaddy rivers. It had been a gruelling march through a night that was black as pitch. So black that the mules had to stand under load when we halted, for had we relieved them of their loads according to rule we should never had succeeded in loading them again.

The going was reasonably good and I remember that we marched with confidence. For some reason there was no need to grope our way: perhaps the denseness of the trees on either side of the track or the ridge that the track followed guided our footsteps. It was not any difficulty that made the march trying but the endlessness of it and the silence and the isolation caused by the unusual absence of light of any sort, for the canopy of the forest shrouded even the glimmer of the stars.

After marching for, I suppose, ten hours one grew aware that dawn was at hand; the figures of the men in front became perceptible and you noticed then that the blackness had turned grey. We halted to close up and to rest the animals and to try to find out where we were. The track which ran along a great limestone escarpment was about to descend into a deep and wide valley across which we had a distant view.

To the north east was a dark mass of tree covered hills silhoutted against a pale sky and as yet formless in the lack of light. As we sat we watched the dawn caress the crest, moulding the tree tops into shape. It was very lovely. The colours in the sky were pale colours, amethyst, amber and jade merging so evenly that they were one. Slowly the light crept down the slope so that the shoulders and spurs stood in relief and cast shadows in the valleys between.

For some days I had felt sure that our track could not be far from that which John's patrol must have used on their way into Burma a year before. All that had happened since pointed to that. The thought recurred to me during the night march and as we sat gazing across the chasm at what now revealed itself to be a romantic tangle of jungle clad hills I told my thoughts to those with me. And even as I spoke conviction grew strong in me so that I said as we rose to go, " I believe that must be the place."

It was the place on which Zaw Gawng put his finger on the map we poured over at Thabeitkyin. It is a place where, rites or no rites, a forester would be glad to lie.

FIFTEEN

AT LAST A VICTORY

by Alister McCrae

It may seem strange to say that I was glad to be back in Burma in January 1944. The war with Japan was still on and the tide had not turned in our favour; certainly not in the Arakan, the theatre to which I was posted. But I had just spent eighteen months in PAIFORCE, the Persia and Iraq Command, where the climate and the endless desert around us had been depressing and unpleasant.

I was one of a number of the British staff of the Irrawaddy Flotilla who had been commissioned into the Indian Army in mid-1942 after we had made our way to Calcutta from a Burma overrun by the victorious Japanese. We were despatched post haste to Basra to join the Inland Water Transport Directorate of the Royal Engineers.

The main task of PAIFORCE at this time was "Aid to Russia" by the Tigris River route and the Persian Railway to the Caspian Sea. We newly joined officers were soon deeply involved in the operation of a hastily requisitioned fleet of elderly local steamers and barges lifting supplies up-river to Kut and Baghdad, and in lighterage in the Persian Gulf ports. At Kuwait, the oil-rich State of today, wooden pontoon barges were being assembled on the beaches for us at the rate of one a day; in those days the fame of Kuwait rested on her just claim to have the finest boat-builders in the Gulf. These barges gave us an immense boost and we were soon handling thousands of tons every day in the ports and up the river. I knew that we were on service vital to the war effort; our Russian ally was in dire need of supplies which only we could get to her. I held a responsible appointment in the rank of Lieutenant Colonel. Yet this was not enough to outweigh the urge to be away from that desert land and back in Burma, to play a part in driving out the Japanese.

I had to ask myself if ten years of living and working in Burma had cast a spell on me, that I was infatuated by so much that Burma gave all of us who came from the West; the beauty

Cox's Bazar
Kalapanzin R.
Bawli Bazar
Naf R.
Buthidaung
Maungdaw
Bay of Bengal
Foul Point
Akyab
ARAKAN

of the land and the waterways, the tinkle of the temple bells, the language with its quaint and intriguing terms of speech. No matter that most of the country was occupied by the enemy, I was glad to be back in that corner of the Arakan which was ours.

I arrived in Chittagong late in January 1944 at the rear H.Q. of the Inland Water Transport Group of which I was to take command, still in the rank of Lieut. Colonel. Chittagong was the supply base for the Arakan forces and my Group were responsible for the port lighterage and the running of coastal steamers south to Cox's Bazaar. A second Group had been operating in the forward area of the Naf River and in the creeks to eastward, but it had been decided that the entire I.W.T. operation should be under one command and I was ordered to take over the lot. This proved to be an experience in itself, for the other Group was commanded by a regular infantry soldier who had acquired no little fame for his exploits in the usually fairly peaceful role of an I.W.T. Group Commander.

Tim Featherstonhaugh had been "discovered" by General Slim after the loss of Burma in 1942, when it was decided that the Sunderbans, delta of the Ganges and Brahmaputra, would have to be patrolled if Calcutta was to be defended. A flotilla of river steamers was gathered and "we found an ideal commander, Lieut. Colonel Featherstonhaugh, a regular soldier who had sailed before the mast, got a coastal mate's certificate and had his wings as an airman. He had led commandos in Norway and was just the man to handle such a military-nautical set-up."* Tim had later moved to command the I.W.T. Group in Arakan.

I went south to take over from him and was given more instruction on the use of the limited small armament on the steamers in the Naf River than on the task before me. His idea of bliss had been to man these personally whenever Jap aircraft came within range. It was just as well to be reminded that the Japanese-held airfield at Akyab was only fifty miles away, but I felt that my experience lent itself more to concentration on the supply operation and less to being a ship's gunner.

The campaign in Arakan had not been a happy one. Having gone there in 1942 as a counter effort to our ignominious defeat earlier that year, the outcome was a second disaster as

**Defeat into Victory* by Field Marshal Sir William Slim, Cassell 1956.

humiliating as the first. Now Arakan had taken on an evil reputation; but the tide was about to turn.

In November 1943 a new offensive was launched by XV Corps under Lieut. General Philip Christison, a great and courageous soldier of wide experience. Again things went badly, but in February 1944 our fortunes changed at last, the Japanese hold in northern Arakan was broken and a great victory won. The Fourteenth Army Commander, General Slim, declared it as the turning point in the whole campaign and "one of the historic successes of British arms". It was a stirring time in which to be involved and to experience for the first time the exhilaration of victory, to be a small part of an army going at last in the right direction. By the time we dug in for the monsoon we were firmly in possession of the whole of Northern Arakan, including the tunnels west of Buthidaung and of Maungdaw and the mouth of the Naf River; all were important to our supply routes.

XV Corps H.Q. was at Bawli Bazaar and it was there I first met Lieut. Colonel Alastair Maclean.[1] He was A.Q.M.G.,[2] and responsible for the supply operation and I was about to have a great deal to do with him. Like the General, Maclean was a Cameron Highlander and one of his accomplishments was the playing of stirring, martial music on his bagpipes. He was glad to find in me a willing listener, for he had rather run out of these at Corps H.Q. Many an evening did we spend with him marching to and fro in front of his basha hut quarters playing "The March of the Cameron Men" and other rousing tunes.

The problem of supplying an army in Burma was more than ordinarily difficult. Such roads as existed in the Arakan were unfit to take heavy vehicles and even an ingenious plan carried out by the Sappers was of limited help. Kilns were set up along the route at twenty mile intervals south into Arakan and the dirt track road bottomed with common bricks. Combined with the I.W.T. coastal and river lift, this took the main burden of supply off the air drop, where another consideration had affected the situation. The aircraft were required to support Chindit operations in Central Burma; and then the rapid advance of the Fourteenth Army (which took them from Imphal across the Chindwin River by early December 1944) was to call for

[1]Brigadier Alastair Maclean was a well known figure in Scotland after the war when for 15 years he was Director of the Edinburgh Military Tatoo.

[2]Assistant Quarter Master General.

increased air supply over a lengthening distance; and as they advanced deeper into Burma that distance would be stretched beyond the limit. General Slim wanted air supply bases nearer Central Burma and these could be provided on the Arakan coast, the first being Akyab. Meantime that brick bottomed road and the I.W.T. had a large supply problem to look after during the 1944 monsoon, and the advance on Akyab was to depend on I.W.T. more than ever. When we had Akyab in our hands, with a port as well as the airfield, our role on coast and river would be over.

The Fourteenth Army advance had begun while the monsoon was still active and General Slim was looking a long way ahead when he gave XV Corps the objective of Akyab as soon as the monsoon was over. Maclean had warned me of the likely part to be played by I.W.T. in this and I was prepared to answer what we could do, and what we could not, when General Christison summoned me to a high level conference that October. There, with his Divisional and Brigade Commanders, the Navy and the R.A.F., the plan for the taking of Akyab was unfolded. It was timed to begin in early December, when we could depend on a season of fine weather. The 25th Indian Division, supported by two West African Divisions, were to attack south down the Mayu peninsula, one Brigade being supplied entirely by sea. This was to be the real testing of us, but I was prepared for it and accepted the task.

I had consulted my Marine Staff Officer, Captain Stewart Knowles, a Hooghly pilot in civilian life, and we had decided to use a number of LCMs (Landing Craft Maintenance) which we were already operating in the wide Naf River estuary. The LCM was a small type of landing craft built of timber and with a stiffened timber ramp. We would load up at Maungdaw and work down the coast, discharging on the beaches as the advance progressed for the fifty miles to Foul Point. By December the calm sea of the north-east monsoon should be established.

My I.W.T. Group advance H.Q. had been set up at Maungdaw, near the mouth of the Naf River, well before the thrust for Akyab began. We were involved during November in the gathering in there of some six hundred country boats of all shapes and sizes, including even sampans; and as soon as Buthidaung on the Kalapanzin River was re-taken these were lifted there by road through the tunnels to carry supplies forward for the West Africans. The use of boats in the Arakan campaign was nothing new. We had specialised Country Craft Companies of around three hundred men, mostly Chittagonians, within the Group, operating in the smaller and otherwise inaccessible creeks.

The south-west monsoon was well spent early in December when XV Corps began the push for Akyab. Knowles and I were at Maungdaw when the first sorties of LCMs went off into the open sea to deliver Brigade supplies to an unsheltered beach. The day was perfect. A gentle breath of air was scarcely perceptible and the sea a flat calm, reflecting the cloudless blue sky. Far to the south we could see the beaches edged with a line of white surf which sparkled in the sun. There was nothing in that peaceful scene to trouble us.

Then came the shock. The LCM Company Commander wirelessed that he was returning without discharging his load, and his report when he arrived back astonished us and caused us no little dismay. Close to the beaches strong undercurrents were at work, an undertow which could pound the lightly built LCMs to pieces. It could be an aftermath of the stormy south-west monsoon, which no doubt would in due course recede. But the advance had started and there was no other means immediately at our disposal to supply that Brigade.

I decided that Knowles and I must investigate ourselves before telling Maclean that some alternative would have to be found. I shuddered to think what General Christison would say: he had entrusted this job to me and I began to visualise the whole operation collapsing because of our failure.

We were off at dawn the next day, Knowles in a sturdy Eureka motor-boat, myself by jeep with my orderly-cum-driver, to rendezvous at a point on the coast some twenty miles to the south. This was further south than where the LCMs had made their attempt, at a creek estuary where shelter from the undertow might be possible. Knowles would see the prospects with his experienced mariner's eye and I would examine the creek. Hopefully we could decide there and then if an LCM could safely beach at that point.

I made first for Brigade H.Q. in a tiny village a few miles south of Maungdaw and told the Brigadier what I intended to do. He showed no enthusiasm at all for my plan, telling me that the rendezvous I had selected was at least a mile beyond his foremost defended position on the coast. This he had just established and what lay beyond was unknown, but was still Japanese held territory as far as he was concerned.

All the persuasion that I was capable of went into convincing that Brigadier that I must get to my rendezvous. My entire plan depended on it, to say nothing of his own Brigade's supplies. We had to determine at once whether or not these LCMs could do the job. Eventually consent was given to my onward journey on condition that an armed escort accompanied me. He gave an order and soon a Sikh havildar with two of his men were climbing noisily into the back of my jeep, clattering their rifles and heavy boots.

We set off on a dusty track and after half an hour of bumping along, turned west for the coastline across uncultivated dry paddy fields. As we drew up a young British officer appeared. He had received notice of our coming and proceeded to tell me where he reckoned the nearest Jap position was, on a knoll to the south-east about a mile inland. His Company of Baluchis was spread out behind a line of scrub holding the Brigade's position close to the coast. He said I must leave the jeep and make for my rendezvous to the south along the shore on foot. If anything started up he would do his best to give us cover.

With my three stalwart Sikhs I marched along the rough shore. On that beautiful morning, with the apparently calm blue sea of the Bay of Bengal stretching to the horizon, it was hard to believe that a problem existed. But it did, and as we marched I could see the undertow in the sea as the short swell developed and broke on the pebbly beach. Our timing was good. There was Knowles in his Eureka running slowly down a quarter of a mile off shore. He hove to and waved as we came to our rendezvous at the creek mouth. The hope that we should find sufficient shelter to bring in the LCMs there was soon dashed when I saw that this typical coastal creek was heavily silted up at the mouth and quite inaccessible. The whole coastline was on a gradual decline and the Eureka was unable to come in closer in safety than two to three hundred yards.

Communication with Knowles at that distance was impossible, with the short surge of the sea on to the shore creating enough noise to make even shouting ineffective. I was deeply worried and wanted to be sure that Knowles agreed with me that the use of the LCMs was impossible; and having no idea of his swimming capabilities, I made a quick decision. There was nothing else for it, I would have to swim out to him. I was a strong swimmer and could see no reason to hesitate.

Telling my havildar that I would be back shortly I stripped off and swam out to the Eureka. If the Japs were watching they must have wondered what was going on. Perhaps the next move would really have puzzled them; it did my escort, crouched on the shore watching the performance. Having conferred with Knowles and decided that some other plan would have to be made and the sooner we were back in Maungdaw the better, I got back into the water and began to swim ashore. On the way out I had realised that the undertow of current was helping me, but I was surprised at the effect it had on my attempt to swim against it. Soon I realised that I would probably drown myself if I went on. I hailed the Eureka, swam back to her and clambered aboard again. I waved to the little group on the shore dutifully awaiting my return, signing that they were to go back to Brigade H.Q. The Eureka swung round and headed north and I saw with relief that they had picked up my clothes and were marching back along the shore.

There was some short-lived amusement when I appeared back at Brigade clad in nothing but a borrowed jungle green army pullover. The escort had returned and I was glad to get dressed again and recover some of my tarnished dignity. I broke the bad news to the Brigadier and promised that something would be done, although I then had no idea what that could be.

The end of the tale is that the situation was saved by the immediate consignment from Calcutta of a number of amphibious vehicles known as "ducks", in army parlance D.U.K.W.S. They did the job, operating on the shoreline and crossing the creeks with impunity. The supply to the Brigade was assured and I breathed again. The 25th Division had advanced to the tip of the Mayu peninsula before the end of December and Akyab was taken without opposition on 2nd January 1945. The Japanese had fled.

That date has a significance. The brilliant campaign of the Fourteenth Army which followed the crossing of the Chindwin early in December brought them to the Irrawaddy just a month later. Akyab was ours to provide the base for the air drop into Central Burma. The recapture of Rangoon before the south-west monsoon broke again in May not only became a possibility; it was achieved. When he summed it up after that great victory, the Supreme Commander, Admiral Lord Louis Mountbatten, wrote:

> "The Burma Campaign has not been simply a battle against a cunning and fanatical foe, but a battle against nature, a battle in which *supplies* were always the deciding factor."

Twenty years later, Alister McCrae on a visit to Burma with Saw Po Hla, pre-war Karen colleague in the Irrawaddy Flotilla Company, gallant comrade of the legendary Major Hugh Seagrim in the Karen Hills during the Japanese occupation.